More Praise for *Changing My Mind*

"It's messy. It's moving. It's playful and a bit cranky . . . but it's *faithful*. Replete with all-too-real anecdotes and the exegetical zeal of decades of ordained ministry, Willimon's *Changing My Mind* is the book about ministerial vocation I didn't know I needed."
    —Rev. Nelson Cowan, Ph.D., United Methodist elder, ordained in 2020, and Director of the Center for Worship and the Arts at Samford University

"*Changing My Mind* is a must-read for every pastor and for those discerning a call into ministry. Part memoir and part epistle, Willimon offers both a word of encouragement to pastoral leaders at the edge of burnout and a constructive critique to those tempted to greatness —reminding each end of that spectrum of Paul's admonition to Timothy to continually 'stir up the gift of God within you.'"
    —Rev. R. DeAndre Johnson, Memorial Drive United Methodist Church, Houston, TX

"*Changing My Mind* is a profound and necessary exploration of an often-overlooked virtue in ministry: the willingness to be transformed. With his characteristic blend of wit and theological depth, Willimon reminds us that the call to ministry is not a call to certainty, but to a dynamic and evolving relationship with God, where our minds, hearts, and ministries are continually reshaped by the

Spirit. In a world that often values rigid conviction over humble growth, Willimon's reflections are a timely reminder that true faithfulness lies in our ability to change our minds in light of God's ongoing revelation."

—Rev. Matt Rawle, Lead Pastor, Asbury United Methodist Church, Bossier City, LA; author of *Jesus Revealed: The I Am Statements in the Gospel of John*

"Longevity in ministry has a way of turning leaders complacent, over-confident, unadventurous, and less curious. Significant experi-ences of God and church are often in the past tense instead of the present. *Changing My Mind* is an antidote to those temptations. Reading it, I was simultaneously convicted, comforted, challenged, and reconnected to the root of my call all while laughing out loud at Willimon's knack for putting into words what so many of us pastors feel in our spirits. If you are feeling stuck in ministry, or want to make sure you don't get there, this book will be a gift to you."

—Rev. Matt Miofsky, Lead Pastor, The Gathering, St. Louis, MO; author of *Let Go* and *The Methodist Book of Daily Prayer*

Will Willimon

CHANGING
MY MIND

The Overlooked Virtue
for Faithful Ministry

 Abingdon Press

CHANGING MY MIND:
THE OVERLOOKED VIRTUE FOR FAITHFUL MINISTRY

Copyright © 2024 by Abingdon Press

ISBN: 9781791033880
Library of Congress Control Number: 2024944061

MANUFACTURED IN THE UNITED STATES OF AMERICA

Again, to Patsy,
about whom my mind has never changed.

CONTENTS

From Paul, who is an apostle of Jesus Christ by the command
of God our savior and of Christ Jesus our hope.
To Timothy, my true child in the faith.
Grace, mercy, and peace from God the Father and
from Christ Jesus our Lord.
—1 Timothy 1:1-2

Preach the word. Be ready to do it whether it is convenient or inconvenient. Correct, confront, and encourage with patience and instruction. . . . Endure suffering, do the work of a preacher of the good news. . . .

Do your best to come to me quickly. Demas has fallen in love with the present world and has deserted me and has gone to Thessalonica. Crescens has gone to Galatia, and Titus has gone to Dalmatia. Only Luke is with me. Get Mark, and bring him with you. . . .

When you come, bring along the coat I left with Carpus in Troas. Also bring the scrolls and especially the parchments. Alexander, the craftsman who works with metal, has really hurt me. The Lord will pay him back for what he has done. But watch out for him, because he opposes our teaching.

No one took my side at my first court hearing. Everyone deserted me. I hope that God doesn't hold it against them! But the Lord stood by me and gave me strength, so that the entire message would be preached through me and so all the nations could hear it. . . . To him be the glory forever and always. Amen.

Say hello to Prisca and Aquila and the household of Onesiphorus. . . .

Try hard to come to me before winter. Eubulus, Pudens, Linus, Claudia, and all the brothers and sisters say hello. The Lord be with your spirit.

Grace be with you all.
—2 Timothy 4:2, 5, 9-11, 13-19, 21-22

With questions for further reflection from William J. Barber, II,
Nadia Bolz-Weber, Jason Byassee, Gabby Cudjoe Wilkes, Kate Bowler,
Lillian Daniel, Lesley Francisco McClendon, Jason Micheli,
Joni S. Sancken, and Jonathan Wilson-Hartgrove.

INTRODUCTION

So God called you to expend your life as somebody's pastor? Put on your oxygen mask before attempting to help others. Fasten your seatbelts, prepare to relocate, hit the road, and itinerate. Peripatetic Jesus loves taking you places you would have never gone had the going been up to you, assigning tasks way beyond your abilities, introducing you to people who, on your own, you might have avoided. You've been warned: Go with Jesus, there'll be bumps. But what a ride.

Can I help?

Timothy, my child, I'm giving you these instructions . . . (1 Timothy 1:18).

Although I'm no Paul and you're not Timothy, what I'm hoping to do is akin to Paul's mentoring of a young colleague in First and Second Timothy. Induction into the craft of ministry is by apprenticeship, a novice looking over the shoulder of a seasoned practitioner, an experienced pastor caring enough about the Body Christ to stand aside and give way to the next generation of Christian leaders.

Many scholars question how the historical Paul of Corinthians and Romans could have written First and Second Timothy. I neither know enough to enter into that debate nor see why it's relevant to my purposes. Though I occasionally note the tension between what Paul says to Timothy and what he says elsewhere, when I refer to "Paul," it's to the perhaps pseudonymous Paul, or the admiring personifier of Paul in First and Second Timothy, who continues to be more Paul than we can handle.

Paul says that he writes to Timothy *if I'm delayed, you'll know how you should behave in God's household* (1 Timothy 3:15). Is "delayed" a euphemism for impending execution?

I shall be "delayed," not by Roman jail but by age from participation in the church you will serve. Though I can't see details of how your church will be different from the church that was so generous to me, I hope my advice will help you figure out *how you should behave in God's household.*

To receive the most from this book of a letter that I'm writing to you, why not read both Timothy letters, start to finish? How about asking a ministerial friend to join you in thinking about ministry along with me, you, Paul, and Timothy?

From Paul, who is an apostle of Jesus Christ by the command of God our savior and of Christ Jesus our hope. To Timothy, my true child in the faith (1 Timothy 1:1-2).

My seminarian's glance at First and Second Timothy was clouded by Rudolf Bultmann's *Theology of the New Testament* (vol. 2). Bultmann trashed the letters as "faded Paulinism," accusing Paul of demoting his gospel to "the framework of Bourgeoise living." Too little existential *Sturm und Drang* for a Marburg professor. Later I learned that was only one of the things Bultmann got wrong.

Timotheos is a pagan name for "One who honors God." A third-generation Christian, Timothy received his faith from women, his mother Eunice passing on what she received from his grandmother Lois—Jesus offered by one generation to another, sort of like what I'm attempting to do to you (Psalm 145:1).

Paul declared that when it came to missionaries, there was nobody like Timothy (Philippians 2:19-24). Timothy's name crops up often as envoy and letter carrier (Acts 17:14-15; Romans 16:21; 1 Corinthians 4:17; 1 Thessalonians 1:1). When things needed sorting in the hot mess at First Church Corinth, who did Paul send? Timothy (1 Corinthians 4:16-17; 16:10-11). During the nearly two decades that they worked together, Paul deployed Timothy to put out (or to ignite) fires all over Asia Minor.

In Thessalonians, Paul called Timothy his "brother" (1 Thessalonians 3:2), in Romans he's a "coworker" (Romans 16:21) but now Timothy is his "child" (1 Timothy 1:2, 18; 2 Timothy 1:2; 2:1). Sounds sentimental to call a grown man a *teknon*, a *dear child*. This unashamedly familial language about a protégé hints at the oddness of Christian leadership. From the first, the church made leaders through affectionate apprenticeship, old guys foisting advice upon the kids whether they wanted it or not. What could I do but delay my retirement and write this letter of a book to you? Thanks for listening.

These letters succinctly reiterate the core of the faith: *This saying is reliable and deserves full acceptance: "Christ Jesus came into the world to save sinners"—and I'm the biggest sinner of all* (1 Timothy 1:15), urge Timothy to be an example for the believers *through your speech, behavior, love, faith, and by being sexually pure* (1 Timothy 4:12), and warn to *watch out* for troubled, troubling church members (2 Timothy 4:15). That's what I want to do for you.

To be honest, Paul's wisdom to Timothy is also peppered with wacky Pauline pet peeves: A wife *should learn quietly with complete submission. I don't allow a wife to teach or to control her husband. Instead, she should be a quiet listener* (1 Timothy 2:11-12). There's also embarrassing apostolic self-justification, chest thumping, score settling, and bridge burning: *Alexander, the craftsman who works with metal, has really hurt me. The Lord will pay him back for what he has done. But watch out for him . . .* (2 Timothy 4:14-15).

I bring up this epistolary quirkiness, not to disparage Paul but to warn that my mentoring, as Paul's, is bound to be a mixed bag. Like Timothy, you must sift the wise counsel from the aged bluster, the useful spiritual guidance from my elderly insistence—on my way out the door—to watch your back; Alexander the craftsman has been a member of every church I've served, seminary faculties too.

I was appointed to be a preacher and apostle of this testimony—I'm telling the truth and I'm not lying! I'm a teacher of the Gentiles in faith and truth (1 Timothy 2:7).

Paul speaks as one under orders, accountable to a message that's neither self-produced nor self-sustained: *I was appointed a messenger, apostle, and teacher of this good news* (2 Timothy 1:11).

Reservations? May you never get over your nagging fear that the job is too big for you; a contented, self-assured pastor could be one who has given up too soon. Reluctant saint, Dorothy Day, in *The Long Loneliness*, which I hope you've read, praises those who "live in a state of permanent dissatisfaction with the Church."[2] To not be a bit ashamed of the present church is indecent. I'm grateful for your desire to change the church and set it to rights. I expect that eventually you'll become more grateful that the church is not worse than it is, but I don't want you to think that too early. If God had not sent you, the church would be worse than it is.

Just a bit younger than I, Augustine, in his *Retractions*, reviewed all that he had written just in case there was anything therein that "offends me or might offend others." My motivation, for this late-in-life retrospective, is not worry over possible offence. God delivered me of that anxiety on my sullen drive from my first church to my second. I look back to help you look forward.

I've been at it for five decades (!) so I've a healthy respect for the perils of the daunting task God has set before you. While I don't know everything about Christian ministry, there's a good chance that my experience has equipped me to be helpful. For decades I've launched scores of new pastors in my Introduction to Ordained Ministry class at Duke. Since the publication of *Pastor: The Theology and Practice of Ordained Ministry*, I've had a hand in the birth of thousands of church leaders in seminaries around the world and have remained a mentor to many.[3]

Can I help you find your own way to serve the servants of God?

I'm reminding you to revive God's gift that is in you through the laying on of my hands. God didn't give us a spirit that is timid but one that is powerful, loving, and self-controlled. . . . Make an effort to present yourself to God as a tried-and-true worker, who doesn't need to be ashamed but is one who interprets the message of truth correctly (2 Timothy 1:6-7; 2:15).

In the antediluvian days when I attempted to steady myself in the face of an impending summons to ministry, an aged pastor (had to be fifty), after listening to my account of my calling, leaned in so close I could smell the garlic and, punching his finger into my chest, said, "Son, if there's any way that you can avoid this, run. Go into the ministry only if there's nothing else you can do."

Callow kid, I thought his was good advice; it was what I was already thinking.

My mind changed. These days, when I meet one thrashing in the throes of to-be-ordained-or-not quandary, I say, "Who knows if God is calling you? Still, on the basis of my life as a pastor, pray hard for God to want you. It's a great way to go."

Will Willimon
The Fifty-Second Anniversary of My Ordination

In the chapters that follow, the statements in the boxes at the beginning are my thoughts before church changed my mind.

The questions in the boxes at the end of the chapter are posed by younger friends of renown to provoke critical dialogue with a new generation of church leaders.

IT'S A JOY TO BE CALLED

> Though pastoral ministry is an arduous, embarrassing, impossible job that no sane person would desire, I liked thinking about God and was good at being good. Loved my youthful experience of church. Enjoyed working with people. Comfortable manipulating older adults.
>
> As campus politician, I was good at public speaking and enjoyed being in front of an audience.
>
> Grateful for the church's participation, such as it was, in the Civil Rights movement.
>
> So there was nothing left for me to do but to be a preacher.

From earliest childhood, I was God curious. Spiritually inclined, I guess you would say. Bible stories, read by my mother each morning at breakfast, were some of the most deliciously violent, perplexing, truthful, occasionally salacious tales anybody dared tell a kid. The bloodier the better. An eight-year-old's day that begins with a boy slingshot conking a giant with a rock, decapitating him, and bragging about it to his buddies, is a day off to a good start.

Our big, rambling downtown Methodist church was filled with interesting, strange, and benign grownups many of whom knew my name even if they weren't Willimons. "Sacristy rat" was Martin Luther's name for kids like me with nothing better to do than hang out at church. While I was working on my God and Country award for Scouts, the preacher slipped me grownup books about Methodists suffering in Cuba or refusing to fight in World War II. There was a day when Methodists were not monotonous?

Ignorant of Paul's warning to Timothy to *Run away from adolescent cravings* (2 Timothy 2:22), I eagerly signed up for church camp. The last night, holding hands and singing *Kumbaya* as we floated candles on paper plates onto the lake was as close to God and a girl as a thirteen-year-old male could get in those days.

At Wofford, religion classes were the most interesting, chock full of critical thinking and illicit ideas. Courageous clergy on the front lines of Civil Rights impressed me and suggested a way to atone for being bred South Carolina guilty. Look! A clerical collar at our antiwar rally; who says clergy are irrelevant? One night in a smoky motel room in Columbia, one of those protesting parsons told stories of otherwise moderate Methodists stomping out in a huff during an abrasive sermon, or a redneck throwing a brick through the back window of a preachermobile in the church parking lot during an NAACP meeting.

"This is great," mused my sophomoric mind. "Where do I sign up?" Yale Divinity, make me a Bible-toting, Scripture-slinging prophet.

A few years into ministry I learned, when it comes down to it, as it always does in the empirical church, *none of this is good enough reason to be a pastor.*

Loving family, positive church experiences, spiritual inclinations, innate talents, and social justice yearnings can't keep you in ministry past your second difficult congregation. The only justification for church, the sole rationale for ministry, is named Trinity. Ministry makes sense only if it's God's idea before yours.

Paul, who is an apostle of Jesus Christ by the command of God our savior and of Christ Jesus our hope (1 Timothy 1:1).

Nobody, not Paul, Timothy, or you can choose to be a pastor. Vocation is not volunteering. You can't aspire for this job; it must be thrust upon you, your personal limitations, reservations, history, or quirks be damned. It's the sort of job that chooses you and, if it works, it fits so well that you think you chose it. Neither career nor profession; as Paul tells Timothy, ministry is at the behest of the world's true "savior" and only "hope" and thus it is called vocation.

Summoned

The Calling of Peter and Andrew, Duccio di Buoninsegna,
The National Gallery of Art, Washington.

What's on your wall? Duccio's *Calling of Peter and Andrew* has been with me since my first day of ministry. Jesus reaches toward two fishermen in their boat. One seems puzzled by the Stranger's reach toward them, the other surprised, looking up from hauling in the nets. The sea roiling with realistic fish contrasts with the mystical, shimmering gold background. Heaven meets earth, two fishermen's every day, workaday world is about to be rocked by the summons of one as yet unknown.

The action, the initiation of the drama, is in the Stranger who calls from the shore. Scant detail, no context or hints at the background or character of the fishermen, as if to say that nothing about them, their identity or personal circumstances accounts for what's happening.

Before Jesus preaches, heals, teaches, or scolds, he calls. The Jesus way of salvation begins with unsettling vocation: a pleasant day of fishing, a thriving family business, four placid, productive, fulfilling lives, wrecked by the call of Jesus:

From that time Jesus began to announce, "Change your hearts and lives! Here comes the kingdom of heaven!" (Matthew 3:2).

As Jesus walked alongside the Galilee Sea, he saw two brothers, Simon, who is called Peter, and Andrew, throwing fishing nets into the sea, because they were fishermen. "Come, follow me," he said, "and I'll show you how to fish for people." Right away, they left their nets and followed him. Continuing on, he saw another set of brothers, James the son of Zebedee and his brother John. They were in a boat with Zebedee their father repairing their nets. Jesus called them and immediately they left boat and father and followed (Matthew 4:18-22).

First word of Jesus: "Change!" All the Gospels begin with similarly disruptive, vocational stories of Jesus breaking the hearts of first-century families by stealing their beloved. Why can't the kingdom of heaven come without upsetting the hell out of kinfolk? I don't know. Couldn't Jesus call us to "comfort," or "care" rather than "Change," then "Come, follow"?

If Jesus, Son of God, wants God's will to be done on earth as in heaven, how come he refuses to do it without these uncredentialled, untrained, unenlightened, and (as we shall discover in the rest of the Gospel) remarkably untalented, knuckleheaded fisher folk nobodies?

What if the time were not right for James and John to walk out on the family business? I bet the Fifth Commandment would have something to say about reckless disregard for the care of aging parents.

Neither Matthew nor Duccio has interest in the backstories of Jesus's calling of disciples. We, who ascribe our lives to urges arising from within us rather than words spoken to us, speculate: Perhaps Peter and Andrew were bored by fishing? It's honorable work, but deadly routine. Surely there's more to life than mending your nets? Perhaps the brothers had conflict with father Zeb over the future of their family fishing business? It happens. What wounds and misfortunes might they have suffered that led them to hope for more fulfilling lives in the Kingdom of Heaven, Inc.?

Well, if they were bored, wounded, or restless, Matthew couldn't care less. It's not the beloved American narrative of fed-up people seeking happier lives, breaking free and hitting the road in pursuit of themselves. It's a bare-bones account of Jesus bent to get back what belongs to God, pausing beside the sea to call, without introduction or explanation, four unlikely people to abandon Dad, throw caution to the wind, and hit the road in service to the Jesus Revolution.

I'm telling you that the story's main actor, the One who sets all in motion, the most outrageously interesting character, is preacher Jesus: "Ready or not, here comes God and there goes you!"

Or as seasoned Paul put it to novice Timothy, you are here not because of who you are but because of who God has called you to be: *God is the one who saved and called us with a holy calling. This wasn't based on what we have done, but it was based on his own purpose and grace that he gave us in Christ Jesus before time began. . . . I was appointed a messenger, apostle, and teacher of this good news* (2 Timothy 1:9, 11). To be blunt, you and I are less interesting than the God who calls us. You don't explain yourself as well as the One who makes your life count through vocation.

In calling his disciples, importunate Jesus doesn't pause to define "kingdom of heaven" or even hint at the direction of the journey. "Here comes God," isn't much of a sermon. Because the meaning has more to do with the Messenger than the message, he calls you not to affirm a philosophy or accept a world view but to risk a relationship.

With the briefest command (or, if you prefer, invitation), "Come, follow me," and an enigmatic promise to train in people-catching, Jesus offers lives we could not have created on our own. *Come*: relocate, be homeless, venture forth to God knows where. *Follow*: submit to walking where and as I walk. *Me*: risk a life in service to a Savior whom you just met.

And you thought your call was unique.

Wonder of wonders, against all odds, they follow. They didn't go looking for Jesus; they simply said, "Yes," when Jesus went looking for them. No search for more fulfilling lives. No tortured discernment or intellectual wrestling ("immediately"). It's a story about the first day of the Jesus Revolution and the weird assemblage he deputizes to fish for others to join the fracas.

Calls the stranger from the shore, "I'm turning the world upside down, inside out, and forcing cosmic regime change. Guess who's going to help me?"

Don't miss the pain behind, "immediately they left. . . ." In saying yes to Jesus, there is also relinquishment. Nobody walks with Jesus without letting go of somebody, somewhere, or something. Boats, nets, father (and for all I know, families too) left behind. Celsus, Roman critic of early Christians excoriated Jesus fanatics for encouraging nice Roman lads to disobey their parents. Romans didn't persecute Christians because they worshipped Christ but because they refused any longer to bow to Caesar. No saying yes to Jesus without saying no to some other competing godlet.

Stop right now. Count up what you gave up in order to walk the way of Jesus. My short list of repudiations: unencumbered time with family, two vacations cut short, a lucrative career as president of Microsoft, being a Republican senator, having everyone with whom I work appreciate me and all I say, a fat honorarium for a humdinger of a homophobic homily at the Faith and Family National Convention. I could go on.

At hearing the Stranger on the Shore call, "Come, follow me," surely the fisher folk responded, "Couple of questions (since this is only the fourth chapter of the Gospel and you have yet to preach or do anything), 1. Who are you? 2. Where are you going?"

That's discipleship. Most of us stumble after Jesus without fully knowing his identity or much less where he's taking us. Be honest now, would you have said yes if you had known what Jesus had in mind for you? Expect surprises. Here's a journey that few want to walk, and nobody can control. And when the way is hard—which (twelve chapters later) he promised it would be (Matthew 16:24-26), and a couple of years hence ends at the Place of the Skull—Jesus shows little sympathy for our complaints about the risky ride.

Joy

Fortunately for you, God has sent me to tell you that there is joy and powerful freedom in knowing—when you're face-to-face with your unrealized ambitions, ponder the gap between your salary compared with what it ought to be, when you stand accused before some snarling church official or crabby congregational board, or quake at a high-paying parishioner's disgruntlement—they don't own you.

As much as any people-pleasing-pastor, or sycophantic cleric, you would like to get along with everybody. But because of vocation, you grovel not for their praise nor are you overly troubled by their censure because, while you work with (and sometimes on) them, you don't work for them. You serve best by refusing to be servile. Your Boss—the one in the front office with a constant, critical eye on your work, and unrealistic expectations for your productivity—is the One who got you into this in the first place.

Vocation.

Thus, when an irate congregant roughed me up after service, fuming about my disgracefulness, how dare I say what I said, and opining that I was nuts to presume that a person such as I should be a pastor in the first place, I replied (in love), "Take it up with the Lord! This is God's idea of a good time, not mine. You think I would have chosen to be here, haranguing the likes of you had the choosing been left up to me?"

Paul blames both his professional sorrows and joys on God: *God is the one who saved and called us with a holy calling. This wasn't based on what we have done, but it was based on his own purpose and grace that he gave us in Christ Jesus before time began* (2 Timothy 1:9).

Nor would I waste your time by asking how you feel about God's decision to expend your life in this way. You've probably already found that your feelings, misgivings, and preferences are quite beside the point when it comes to ministry. In vocation, God's "purpose" and "grace" call the shots.

Timing not right? Reservations about your gifts for this line of work? Parents planned and paid for a different life trajectory? Not good on your feet? Fear of public speaking? Shy? Prone to depression?

God doesn't care. God calls whom God chooses. Recall the inscrutable summons of Jacob, Abraham and Sarah, Peter and Paul. "Mary, how did you decide that being impregnated by the Holy Spirit out of wedlock in order to bear God's Son was a good fit for you?"

Get my drift?

You may have limitations and quirks, but don't flatter yourself. Yours are no worse than theirs. Look what God did through them, in spite of them. In your qualms about submitting to the yoke of obedience, the service of the Word, administration of the sacraments, and the care of God's people, take heart: The God of Israel and the church is a sucker for losers, lost causes, and delights in throwing people into water that's way over their heads. Read the Bible. *Don't be ashamed of the testimony about the Lord or of me, his prisoner. Instead, share the suffering for the good news, depending on God's power* (2 Timothy 1:8).

Don't you find it remarkable that Paul tells Timothy that he is a "prisoner," not of the empire in whose jail cell he languishes, but of the Lord? Paul doesn't say his "suffering" is due to the lack of Roman religious pluralism or overreach of Caesarian colonialism. He's in this fix because of "the good news," blaming the trauma of his incarceration, the misery of his situation, on Jesus.

Sunk in despair over the state of one of my congregations, I poured out my heart to my kindly but decrepit (the man had to be sixty, at least) district superintendent. I was hoping for him to pull a *Deus ex machina* (I was so dumb about DS's back then). All he did was to lend a sympathetic ear and then to say unctuously, "Son, isn't it reassuring that God will never allow anything worse to happen to you in ministry than he allowed to happen to his own Son?"

Feel better now? In a way, I did.

A sociologist (!) at the divinity school led a discussion, "Dealing with Toxic, Difficult Laypeople." I reassured students, "Don't bother. Today's laity are so disorganized, they have forgotten how to kill a Methodist preacher; a fat pension and insurance are as effective. I've served some of the sorriest, meanest congregations the Lord ever created and I can tell you, your problem won't be difficult laity, it will be demanding Jesus."

There. Does that help?

Paul pulls no punches. Did a chill go down young Timothy's spine when he heard mentor Paul speak of his suffering and imprisonment? *You have seen me experience physical abuse and ordeals in places such as Antioch, Iconium, and Lystra* (2 Timothy 3:11).

As a teenager I believed that vocation was adequately described by our church's Director of Christian Education's slogan, "Where the needs of the world and your talents meet, that's your vocation." I even believed, for maybe nine or ten minutes, Robert Bly's characterization of vocation as "follow your bliss." Now I know I was wrong. Nothing is able to sustain ministry when it causes you little bliss to preach the gospel, when it's not personally fulfilling to bury their dead, or walk with some troubled soul through the valley, or when even the sacraments bore you, nothing will keep you alive except the peculiar joy provoked in you by your vocation. You must be convinced that God really is in Word and Sacrament, in your performance of the mundane tasks of raising the dead, healing the sick, casting out demons, turning wine into blood, preaching the truth, and bringing in the kingdom of heaven, or ministry is misery.

God is the one who saved and called us with a holy calling. This wasn't based on what we have done, but it was based on his own purpose and grace that he gave us in Christ Jesus (2 Timothy 1:9).

I've known people who have drifted into the insurance business; nobody ever floated toward ministry. You must be called. What joy in that. On Sunday—when you put on your alb (covering Saturday's ketchup-spotted shirt), pull tight the cincture (though you're not celibate), hang the stole around your neck (which signifies?), and go out there and talk about the God we didn't expect, even when you may not feel like it and many of them don't want to hear it—you've got to believe that somehow Jesus knew what he was doing when he called you. In ways you'd be the last to know, Jesus's *purpose and grace* are conspiring to call the people he wants to love the world he deserves.

In friend Frederick Buechner's *The Book of Bebb* a has-been, alcoholic preacher, sunk in depression at the state of his life and ministry, is asked by a sympathetic friend, "Why did you keep at it?"[1]

Bebb pounds his fist and snarls, "Because I was called, dammit."

Barna claims that 20,000 pastors took the pandemic as an opportunity to get out of the ministry. Fifty percent of current pastors say they would cut and run if they had another way of making a living.[2] It's my guess that those who stayed have no better reason than, "I was called."

I'm all for measureable results, visible fruit, noting the numbers, going with your gut, and affirming your strengths, but sometimes the only thing that keeps you going is either sheepishly or defiantly (maybe, by God's grace, gratefully) to say, "I was called."

Go ahead, put yourself into situations that are so absurdly ambitious, risky, threatening, and bodacious that when asked, "What are *you* doing *here?*" you have no better explanation than, "Ask Jesus."

The main assignment of the Christian life is to relinquish delusions of self-control and fall into the arms of a merciful God, humbly allowing yourself to be summoned by the Stranger who calls from the shore. The purpose of church is to equip you for the called life. Your point as pastor is to enable the saints to call out to the One who has called to them, to care for those who have been wounded by their vocations, to give the baptized the sustenance they need to stand on the front lines with Jesus, weekly to nourish them with the body and blood of Christ. Ah, those happy few (though they number in the millions) whom Jesus has invited to join him in giving away the good news, getting out of their boat and into his, setting forth on a sometimes turbulent sea, sailing to God only knows where, waiting, working, and praying for his kingdom to come, his will to be done on earth as in heaven.

Bless you for saying yes to the Stranger on the Shore reaching toward your boat that once bobbed aimlessly with the tide. Thanks to his call, you get to row against the stream. Taking your place alongside Paul, Timothy, Peter, and Mary who responded to Christ's call, risk takers with the guts to get in the boat with Jesus, you mumble, "Don't know where you're taking me, much less what the trip will cost, but you might as well count me in."

Questions from Kate Bowler, *New York Times* bestselling author, "Everything Happens" podcaster, and Professor of American Christianity, Duke Divinity School:

1. Our culture wants us to believe that our sacred callings should be another form of matchmaking.

Fill out this questionnaire and you will be paired with someone who shares your values and helps you become your best self. Jesus will find you the congregation of your dreams. Of course, that never happens. Do we need to entirely de-romanticize our callings to hear what God is saying? Or is there a sacred harmony that we should expect when we serve people?

2. Our vocations are supposed to help us grow. What signs should we look for that our calling is helping us become a better self and not simply someone who is surviving where they are placed?

3. Will, does your view of calling end up being totalitarian? I can imagine that this could sound a bit like, "God never gives you a calling you can't handle." Which can't possibly be true—so how can we hold on to this account of calling in a way that doesn't require that to be true?

CHANGING MY MIND

> I need to go to a good seminary where I'll receive a theological foundation that fixes me for years of ministry.
>
> I must learn how to manage and not mess up the healthy congregation that's handed to me for my safe-keeping.

I grew up on red clay, kudzu-overrun dirt that my family had worked for two hundred years, baptized into octagonal McBee Chapel Methodist Church, South (no time, in the twenty years since Methodist merger, to change the denomination's name on the sign out front), eventually confirmed into downtown Buncombe Street Methodist Church (which my buddies nicknamed Jesus National Bank because of its Ionic columned façade). Like many churches, Buncombe Street (so named before H. L. Mencken coined the put-down "bunkum") tried to look two hundred years older than it was, bigger, heavier than needed to con Greenville into thinking that our church had loomed over Buncombe Street, since before The Flood.

How comforting to have something that didn't change, hadn't so far as I could tell, for maybe a thousand years. The ancient hymns that nobody sang anymore, except for an hour a week at Buncombe Street, and the ponderous church furniture, bolted to the floor, were predictable, reassuring to a kid for whom most days were unexpected.

"Why do you wear a black robe?" I asked, during Dr. Herbert's inquisition by our confirmation class.

He explained, "It's the way educated men dressed a couple of hundred years ago."

Of course.

I'm sure the sheer there-ness, the irrefutable immutability of the church was consoling to a kid in a Southern town that still clung to the Old South but (so I overheard the anxious grownup talk in the church parking lot) was on the brink of alteration.

Christ, Agent of Change

My theory is that churches like Buncombe Street try to look stolid because Jesus isn't. (As theologian Karl Barth said, Christians go to church to make our last stand against a living, unsettling God. Sometimes, the building helps with that.) People say they pay you to bring them closer to God but, the more you get to know them, the more you suspect they secretly hope you'll protect them should God slide in too close. Those who come singing, "Just as I am," inchoately know that Jesus intends never to leave them just as they are.

"The purpose of this class is to acquaint you with the Old Testament so that you can begin to know a people who have known God five thousand years longer than you," said Professor Bullard as he strutted about in the first session of freshman Old Testament. It was my first clue that the purpose of biblical interpretation is not to adapt the Bible to suit the sensibilities of modern people like me but rather to modify people like me so that we're worthy to be in conversation with the Bible.

"In three years we will ground you in a theology that will be an enduringly firm foundation for every turn and twist in your ministry," assured Interim Dean Johnson as he oriented us to Yale Divinity School in the fall of 1968. Amid the killings of King and Kennedy, the

Kent State and Orangeburg massacres, as tear gas mingled with the smell of hemp, it was heartening to hear that we would be theologically funded, formed, and fixed by the time we walked away with a Bachelor of Divinity.

Surprise. The B.D. I planned to receive was discarded by the school before I could get one and replaced by the shiny new M.Div. That should have cautioned me about transmogrifications that lay ahead. *Gott nimmer ruhet,* God is restless, said Barth. Rabbi Heschel says a biblical prophet is one whom God "stirred."

Church changed my mind: The foundation of the Christian faith is not a good theological standpoint, an immutable worldview, or an eternal-looking sanctuary; there's no other basis than Christ (1 Corinthians 3:11), a living person moving toward us, not a set of ossified propositions ventured by us.

Another decade of ministry passed before I learned that you can tell a dead god (idol) from the true, living God by the way an idol—your own sweet concoction—neither tells you anything you wouldn't tell yourself, nor tries to revise you.

Christians believe in something because we have been encountered by Someone. Jesus, tell us some truth: Jesus answers, "I am the way, the truth, and the life. No one comes to the Father except through me" (John 14:6). A person, a Jew from Nazareth who lived briefly, died violently, and rose unexpectedly, that's truth?

With the resurrected Christ, truth personified, we've got more tomorrows than yesterdays with him. It's futile to try to go back and reconstruct facts about Christ that are more real than the Jesus who is with us in the present, personally self-revealing anew, telling us things he didn't have time to tell us before we tried to shut him up. See him striding, always, into the future, truth forever beyond our grasp. "Follow me." If we are to be with Truth-in-Person, we must stumble after him, as he's always pioneering ahead (Hebrews 12:2).

Time and again, when I've arrogantly thought myself to be working solo, Christ showed up, forcing me to join in Jacob's, "The LORD is definitely in this place, but I didn't know it" (Genesis 28:16).

I left seminary presuming I had a bag of tricks, an ordered, reliable theology. All I needed was to return South, repackage my theology and put it on the bottom shelf for lay consumption.

But then, in the daily collusion (sometimes collision) between Christ and his church, I was compelled to refocus, retrofit, revise, reframe, sometimes even renounce and recant what I once knew for sure.

Seminary gave me seat belts for the bumps in the ride ahead, every morning to jump out of bed and say to Jesus, "Tell me again, who are you and how will you modify my plans for today?"

Go to the Wofford College Archives, Willimon Collection, rifle the files of my sermons, decades past, and exclaim, "So you preached a sermon in 1979, 'Discovering a More Positive Self Image'? Wow. You've changed."

There were times when my mind changed because of change in my ministerial context. The culture shifted, the world spun in a different direction, or the bishop plopped me in a place where my previous tricks fell flat. I was forced back to Square One to rethink what I once thought I knew for sure.

In other instances, my mind changed because that's what the Holy Spirit loves to do. A profound instability ensues the moment you're pulled out of the baptismal waters and hands are laid on your head. Everybody who serves Jesus is required to hit the road. Acquiesce to Jesus's "follow me" and you'll find yourself relocating, itinerating, being born again, then again. The Holy Spirit makes intellectual nomads of all upon whom the Spirit descends because God's creative work didn't end with Genesis 1 and 2, and raising the dead is, for Christ, just another day at the office.

My Mind Changed

Bethlehem and Golgotha name how God in Christ enters time, makes time, takes time for us. Nobody can be in history without change. More to the point of Jesus, nobody loves another without changing in order to stay in love with the beloved.

When Patsy and I married and escaped to Yale Divinity School in the summer of '69, I was sure I had married the right person. Not only did I adore her, she also knew more about ministry than I. Nobody in my family had been clergy, whereas in Patsy Parker's family, her grandfather, grandmother (first ordained Methodist woman in South Carolina), and father were preachers. Church, the Parker family business. Patsy, astute post sermon evaluator, though please, not before Tuesday.

But like the week after we married, or maybe the next day, that "right" person changed into another, then changed again. That's what living persons do.

Which explains why the promises of Christian marriage are in the future tense: "Will you love . . . ?" The church, in its wisdom, never asked, "Have you found the one perfect, right person with whom to bed down the rest of your life?"

Rather, the church asks, "Will you promise to love this person through all the changes wrought by time, place, personality, and God 'till death do you part?"

When God promised contingent, sinful Israel, "I'll take you as my people, and I'll be your God" (Exodus 6:7), God spoke in the future tense, forever, freely wedding God's self to us creatures.

Experienced, aging, ex-religious terrorist, six-time-loser, incarcerated Paul becomes a trail guide for Timothy. Paul speaks as one still reeling from his knockdown by the risen Christ on the Damascus Road, Church Enemy Number One changed to Church Planter Par Excellence:

[Christ] appointed me to ministry even though I used to speak against him, attack his people, and I was proud. But I was shown mercy because I acted in ignorance and without faith. Our Lord's favor poured all over me along with the faithfulness and love that are in Christ Jesus. This saying is reliable and deserves full acceptance: "Christ Jesus came into the world to save sinners"—and I'm the biggest sinner of all (1 Timothy 1:12-15).

Remember, Jesus loves to shake aggressive, proud, ignorant, sinners like Paul and me, a thought that may fit you for the changes Christ is sure to work in you. Once Jesus Christ set out to save sinners, he filled the world with folks who, by virtue of their baptism, are given the guts to say to God and neighbor, "I have been revised."

A prominent, seasoned, mature religious leader comes to Jesus by night and interrogates him about his program of eternal life (John 3). "We know that you, . . ." Nicodemus brags about his spiritual insight. With a seeming *non sequitur*, Jesus tells old Nicodemus that he must be born *anothen* (again, anew, shook up from top to bottom).

"How can this be?" the once self-assured, interrogating, knowledge-able, now confused, interrogated, disoriented Nicodemus asks. Who among the mature and knowledgeable wants to be retrofitted into the fetal position, pushed once more unwillingly down the birth canal, smacked on the rear, and then plopped into a world you didn't choose!

Jesus promises (or threatens?) Nicodemus, "*Pneuma* blows where it wants." We have as much say so over the wind as we do over our birth. Uncontained, uncontrollable. You're never so mature, self-confident, experienced, and certain that you are immune from the possibility that the Holy Spirit will blow through your brain, pop you on the rear, as you mutter, "I once thought this way, but now my mind has changed." Flipped, detoxified, reborn, reconfigured by the God who boasts, at the end of the Bible and the beginning of the church, "Look, I'm making all things new" (Revelation 21:5).

The other day, a separating Methodist pompously labeled himself a stand-your-ground "Traditionalist." Knowing that the man had risked baptism, I grinned, "Lots of luck with that."

I hope that you, as a person starting out in ministry, will take com-fort that a crusty, soon-to-be-octogenarian can admit, "My mind was once made up on that subject but now, by the grace of God, God's taken a stronger hand in making up my mind, so here I bear witness that my mind has been changed."

Our forty-fifth president bragged that he would never ask for for-giveness (surprised that he's on his third marriage?). Although many of his supporters have found it tough to confess they were wrong to support a man who, among other failings, refuses to say he was wrong, most of us find that once blindsided by a merciful, forgiving God, we delight in admitting culpability. Every Sunday's worship begins with corporate confession: "Once again, we messed up, goofed, screwed up, and were mistaken. As did our parents and grandparents. Lord, again, forgive us and set us right."

My changes of mind are evidence for the reality of the Third Person of the Trinity, the action of God on the church and a life. Changelessness (*immutabilitas*) was an unfortunate compliment medieval philosophy tried to pay God. While I affirm Hebrews 13:8, Christ is better than immutable; he is the Incarnate One, infinite God taking time for finite us.

Friends sometimes said to me when I became a pastor, "You've changed" or "Please don't change," that is, don't submit to a vocation that could transform you into someone with whom we are uncomfortable.

My home church left The UMC fearing that it would change if it stayed. As W. H. Auden put it, they "would rather be ruined than changed."[1] They will fail to impose stability on Jesus, or to steady the God who makes "all things new" (Revelation 21:5).

I remind you that the story of Jesus begins with a transformational sermon by John the Baptist who "was in the wilderness calling for people to be baptized to show that they were changing their hearts and lives . . ." (Mark 1:4). The Baptizer introduces Christ with a terse, three-point sermon: 1. You are not right as you are. 2. Be baptized. 3. Repent. Nobody comes to Jesus without *metanoia*, metamorphosis (which the Baptizer presents as a post-baptismal experience!).

As Archbishop Rowan Williams said in a sermon, the church is welcoming, but not merely inclusive. Newcomers are welcomed with, "'You can come in, and that decision will change you.' We don't say: 'Come in and we ask no questions.' Conversion means conversion of habits, behaviors, ideas, emotions. The boundaries [of change] are determined by what it means to be loyal to Jesus Christ."[2]

Wesleyans used to be big on conversion, Wesley's heart warmed at Aldersgate, our God-wrought sanctification, changing of heart and mind. Now we've got Methodists who "disaffiliate" out of fear that they might be modified by membership in The UMC. Go figure. They forsake a church that birthed them in order to age as they are. Right-wing politics leveraging fear of divine *metanoia.*

Just remember: any God who would enlist murderer, self-admitted *biggest sinner of all* (1 Timothy 1:16) Saul is just the sort who would summon the likes of you or me. Think that Jesus won't tamper with your self-constructed you? Don't flatter yourself; you are as pliable to God's *metanoia* as Paul's, and your baggage is surely no worse.

Midway through this life's journey I spent two years learning Italian in order to read Dante. The common characteristic of doomed sinners in *Inferno* is that they aren't going anywhere, frozen, enslaved to their sin. Stuck. But when we enter *Purgatorio,* everybody is in motion, on the way, being purged for *Paradisio.* Even Manfred, whom Dante meets at the gates of *Purgatorio,* though twice excommunicated and condemned to hell by no less than two popes, marvels that a forgiving God has nullified the ossifying judgments of the fossilized church, blessing him with the ability to change, moving him ever closer to God, even in death. The resurrection promise? "All of us won't die, but we will all be changed" (1 Corinthians 15:51).

In Acts 9, somebody no one had ever heard of, Ananias, is told to go to Straight Street and lay healing hands on Church Enemy Number One, religious terrorist Saul. Ananias pleads, "Lord, I have heard many reports about this man. People say he has done horrible things to your holy people in Jerusalem" (Acts 9:13), thinking that Christ has given him the wrong name and address. "The Lord replied, 'Go! This man is the agent I have chosen to carry my name before Gentiles, kings, and Israelites. I will show him how much he must suffer for the sake of my name'" (Acts 9:15-16). Saul is healed of his God-woundedness, not in order to free him from pain and disability but rather to induce even greater suffering, now, as agent of Christ. "Saul thinks he's suffered; wait until he works for me," blusters the risen Christ.

Still, be honest. Even in your status quo loving self, isn't there some reckless, secret you that longs to be fitted out and sent to the front lines? Upon hearing Paul's put-down of his former congregation, *some people have been distracted by talk that doesn't mean anything. . . . They are the ungodly . . . sinners . . . people who are not spiritual, and nothing is sacred to them. They kill their fathers and mothers, and murder others. They are . . . sexually unfaithful, and . . . have intercourse with the same sex . . . kidnappers, liars, individuals who give false testimonies in court, and those who do anything else that is opposed to sound teaching* (1 Timothy 1:6, 9-10), for any of your cautious, rule-keeping, churchy niceness you say, "Hey coach, put me in the game, give me the ball."

Kill their fathers and mothers? I've had my share of *liars* and *sexually unfaithful* in my churches but even the worst wouldn't stoop to matricide. Paul must have been one heck of an evangelist.

Or did Paul out these *ungodly . . . sinners* as sly enticement of Timothy into the wild rapids otherwise known as working with Jesus Christ? I see Timothy clenching his fist and muttering, "Attention deficient listeners, ungodly congregants, murderers and adulterers, sexually screwed up saints, kidnappers, liars, this sermon's for you!"

Out of Yale Divinity School and into the South Carolina Conference of The UMC, the bishop found no church equal to my training and talent. Though I complained, the only parishes available were full of white segregationist fools, hell bent on keeping the Twentieth Century out of their church. When I protested the injustice of a pastor like me stuck with losers like them, Bishop Tullis smirked, "Who better to cure their racism than one of 'em? A nicer person wouldn't be up to the task. If the Lord changed a hardhead like you, think what the Lord can do for them. Right?"

Then he added, "I'm from Kentucky. Are you surprised I didn't choose to move here? Like you, I don't care for many of these people. But Jesus Christ thinks they're to die for. Son, *this is the job!*"

Saving Sinners

Once Jesus Christ took as his task the saving of sinners, only sinners, he forever made ministry in his name a risky line of work. Your congregation is homophobic, warring Red against Blue, incipiently white nationalist? It's the job. If you have been wondering, "Why was *I* called into ministry?" look upon the motley crew whom Jesus has assembled; you'll have your answer.

Pray, Jesus urges, God to send more sinners like you to gather God's bountiful, expansive, heterogeneous harvest (Luke 10:2). Look at you, God's answer to somebody's prayer.

The Incarnation is God contextualizing. That's why church leadership books have a short shelf life. "Six Steps Toward Being an Effective Pastor" falsifies the richness and diversity of pastoral contexts, as well as the specific gifts God has given you. I'll therefore not insult your intelligence by giving you detailed prescriptions for how to lead a church. For one thing, your future in ministry is whatever you and the Holy Spirit make of it. For another, you won't be leading the church I served. Improvisation, creativity, and flexibility are the order of the day. So I'll keep hammering the notion that, when you come to a fork in the road and don't know which step to take, it's life or death to be clear about who you are, why you're here, and to whom you're accountable. Then go ahead. Barth's *Church Dogmatics* will be more helpful in keeping you in ministry than books on church management (including the ones I've written). Many of your seminary profs got there because they didn't mind spending some of the best years of their lives alone in the library. Most graduates find themselves reasonably well-equipped to function in a church that no longer exists.

Because pastoral work is public and political, you'll learn how to lead by apprenticing to those who are actually leading in context, learning in the tug-and-pull of our first years after seminary. Yet, choose your mentors carefully.

As bishop, I heard unhappy clergy grouse, "This wasn't the job I signed up for," bewildered that God had changed their context in ways for which they were untrained to lead.

Others excused their ineffectiveness with, "I was raised in a troubled family. I just don't do conflict." Or, "I'm not much of a preacher, but I am a wonderfully attentive pastor." I took this to mean, "I'm too arrogant to submit to learning the skills and making the necessary changes that would enable me to help this congregation have a future."

Ambiguity in Ministry

My nativity was into a culture of legally enforced racial segregation. Every day I boarded a Greenville City Bus (operated by the Duke Power Company) that had a big sign, "White Patrons Sit from the Front, Colored Patrons Sit from the Rear, South Carolina Law." Nobody I knew questioned that sign, least of all, nobody in church.

I've been grateful, yes, that's the word, grateful that I still can recall the segregated church that introduced me to Jesus. It's salubrious to know from the start that it's possible for you, your parents, and yes, even your beloved, innocuous pastor to be wrong.

"Slaves at Worship on a Plantation in South Carolina," *Harper's Magazine,* 1855

Willie Jennings's *After Whiteness* introduced me to an etching of a South Carolina preacher and his 1850's congregation.[3] The preacher stands above them, dressed in the attire of the white master who sits with his family underneath the pulpit. The master holds a Bible in his lap and seems to be listening thoughtfully. Or is he smugly monitoring the preacher, pleased that the preacher is saying nothing out of line? The preacher is dressed differently from most of those in his congregation. Are his fine clothes a sign that the master recognizes the preacher's God-given talent? Or does his clothing indicate the preacher's accommodation to the system of human bondage presided over by his white master? Many in the congregation seem appreciative of the preacher's sermon, but some of the younger folk, toward the back, look uninterested, maybe contemptuous.

We don't know for sure. Is this a depiction of the triumph of the gospel even in the horribly dehumanizing context of enslavement? Or is it a picture of the gospel's perversion by systems of oppression? Is the preacher courageously speaking for God even in a deadly, ungodly context or is he being used as a tool of the ungodly? We don't know, and we doubt the preacher knows for sure.

A chill goes down my spine looking at this etching from long ago. It's a reminder that any preacher can be used for good or ill, may be a rebel against or a conspirator with the powers-that-be, a spokesperson for God or a mouthpiece for the oppressor. Any congregation too.

And yet, maybe we ought to view this image of an enslaved preacher with wonder. We're witnessing a miracle. African Americans, who received the gospel of Jesus Christ from the hands of their white enslavers, said, in effect, "We'll take Jesus, but not your interpretation and the way you live your faith in Jesus." God enabled Christians of color to disentangle the gospel good news from the bad news of our sinful white distortions. It's possible to get God wrong, very wrong but, by the grace of God, it's possible for God to help make it right.

Maybe every time we baptize, we ought to whisper to the new Christian, "Glad to have you aboard. Just remember: while you make your promises to God, the wind blows where it wants and you never get so adept at the gospel that you're too old to be born again. Brace yourself; by the grace of God, you'll be changed."

Questions from Lesley Francisco McClendon, senior pastor of C3 Hampton, a Mennonite Church USA congregation in Hampton, Virginia. Lesley has served as an instructor at Duke Divinity School and the Anabaptist Mennonite Seminary. She is founder of Herstoric, Inc., which provides professional leadership development and coaching for women leaders.

1. Bishop, you mention that the purpose of biblical interpretation is not to adapt the Bible to suit modern sensibilities, but to change people so they're worthy to be in conversation with the Bible. How do you reconcile this view with the need for contextual interpretation of scripture to address contemporary issues and challenges?

2. This chapter raises questions about the nature of truth and the role of interpretation in understanding scripture and tradition. Is there a way preachers can engage with these questions in a manner that is faithful to their tradition and open to new insights? Can we embrace the challenge of change while remaining rooted in our faith and convictions?

3. Although we may not know the full context, the image of the slave preacher highlights the tension between accepting the gospel message and challenging the oppressive systems of the time. How can ministers navigate similar tensions today, where issues of injustice and inequality persist?

PREACHING IS THE MOST IMPORTANT THING YOU DO

> Sure, pastors preach, but mostly they care for the needs of the congregation and work for justice in the wider community. With so many demands on a pastor's time, sometimes preparation for preaching takes a back seat to more relevant responsibilities.
>
> Sermons ought to connect with real people's real problems, building a bridge from the ancient world of the Bible to contemporary concerns, speaking to the great issues of the day, translating the faith into terms that are understandable and useful to modern people.
>
> Sermons encourage Christians to live more fulfilling lives and to make the world a better place.

Summer of 1973, sequestered as associate pastor in remote Clinton, South Carolina, far from the action of Watergate, Washington, and all that, disappointed by my own tepid response to small town racism and eager to do something "relevant," I picked up William Stringfellow's *An Ethic for Christians and Other Aliens in a Strange Land*. An

Episcopal layperson, lawyer, and firebrand activist, Stringfellow had become one of my heroes.

After a scorching indictment of Nixon *et alia* (see why I loved him?) in which Stringfellow came close to calling for an overthrow of "reputed leaders" of government, in a grand crescendo of prophetic indignation he tells the clergy how to foment revolution—preach:

> In the face of death, . . . in the middle of chaos, celebrate the Word. Amidst babel, I repeat, speak the truth. Confront the noise and the verbiage and falsehood of . . . death with the truth and potency and efficacy of the Word of God. Know the Word, teach the Word, nurture the Word, preach the Word, defend the Word, incarnate the Word, do the Word, live the Word. . . . In the Word of God, expose death and all death's works and wiles, rebuke lies, cast out demons, exorcise, cleanse the possessed, raise those who are dead in mind and conscience.[1]

Jesus, the Word, came preaching (Mark 1:14). Although there is much that we don't know about God, one thing we know from Scripture and years of church experience: The triune God is a big talker. Insistently communicative, determined to make verbal contact. The Stranger on the beach who initiated the conversation, keeps calling, commencing, and sustaining colloquy. Although the God of Israel is parsimonious and picky about visual images of God, words from, to, and about God are a deluge, more God-talk than we've ever been able adequately to digest. Creation begins with a sermon, "Let there be light," delivered to dark *tohuwabohu* (Genesis 1:3). God had only to say the word and a new world was preached into being. This verbally dexterous, sometimes even (not to be critical) verbose Creator not only creates, sustains, and redeems the world but insists on telling us all about it. Isn't it a wonder that the Bible is longer than it need be and we preachers never exhaust what could be said about what God has said?

If you haven't already, you will soon find that much of the adventure in ministry is getting to know the Trinity who so cunningly called

27

you. God the Father in constant conversation with God the Son, the Son interacting with God the Father, God the Holy Spirit in the name of the Father and Son relentlessly communing with humanity. Having had the Trinity somehow find a way to reach out to you, in spite of your many defenses, you know that the God of Israel and the church is nothing if not relationally loquacious.

Nobody has ever told the good news to themselves. Thus, from the first, Jesus delegated preaching to those whom he called (Mark 16:15), recklessly telling them "whoever listens to you, listens to me" (Luke 10:16). No way to work for this garrulous God without commission as spokesperson. "Servants of the Word" was Luther's designation for clergy; "mouth house" the ideal Lutheran church.

One of the last things Paul tells Timothy is that of first importance: *Until I arrive, pay attention to public reading, preaching, and teaching. Don't neglect the spiritual gift in you that was given through prophecy when the elders laid hands on you. Practice these things, and live by them so that your progress will be visible to all. . . . If you do this, you will save yourself and those who hear you* (1 Timothy 4:13-16).

Like Timothy you're under orders—by God and the church—to speak up for God. While it's a joy, in this numbingly narcissistic neighborhood, to have something to talk about other than ourselves, it's also a heavy responsibility. Yet, as Karl Barth said, because of the vocative, voluble nature of the God who is, rather than the coy, taciturn, reticent God we wish there were, it's easier for us preachers to tell the truth about God than about ourselves. Our selves are arcane, hidden, and evasive whereas a revelatory God is not.

I was appointed to be a preacher and apostle of this testimony . . . a teacher of the Gentiles in faith and truth (1 Timothy 2:7). Paul enjoys referring to himself as *apostolos*, an "apostle" (*stellein* to send, *apo* off, away from), one who is not preaching on his own but as herald, spokesperson, envoy, ambassador. We preach, not to get something off our chests and not because we're experts on the subject, but because we were sent off.

Preach the word. Be ready to do it whether it is convenient or inconvenient. Correct, confront, and encourage with patience and instruction (2 Timothy 4:2).

Paul tells Timothy, when preaching, to *present yourself to God as a tried-and-true worker, who doesn't need to be ashamed but is one who interprets the message of truth correctly* (2 Timothy 2:15). Care about God's approbation more than your congregation's. Preachers believe that the opposite of love is not insensitivity or indifference, it's lies. We love our people enough to tell them the truth and allow them to tell the truth to us.

God's verdict on our sermons counts more than theirs.

Timothy is warned about people's easy disbelief: *People will not tolerate sound teaching. They will collect teachers who say what they want to hear because they are self-centered. They will turn their back on the truth and turn to myths. But you must keep control of yourself in all circumstances. Endure suffering, do the work of a preacher of the good news, and carry out your service fully* (2 Timothy 4:3-5).

Suffering uncomfortably close, in the same sentence, to *preacher of the good news.*

Speaking Up for God

"Just share yourself," preachers are advised, as if that's enough material for a sermon. "Preach from your personal [Latinx, LBGQT+, white, cisgender, wounded, Midwestern, democratic, and so on] experience." Conventional counsel in a culture that regards personal experience as revelatory and ontologically significant. Trouble is, what counts as, "my experience" is not to be trusted as an accurate rendition of me. Besides, in your sermon you offer listeners an experience (encounter with Christ) they wouldn't have had if you had lacked the guts to speak up for God in a culture that fantasizes that personal experience is God.

When I was starting out, somebody told me that interesting sermons "begin with a question and then offer an answer." Worse, later I was advised, "preach the questions, not the answers."

My mind changed. In the course of my preaching life I found that the gospel is not the answer most hope to hear. Open-ended questions are safer than the answer, "Jesus Christ."

How can I have a more peaceful life? Where can I find healing for my personal trauma and pain? Wherein is peace in an upwardly mobile, privileged, upper middle class, therefore stress-filled world? What's to be done about American, white, Christian racism? Why get out of bed in the morning?

Good questions. Alas, they are of little interest to the gospel of Jesus Christ. I discovered the truth (or, more likely, it found me) that the query of Scripture, and the good news borne by the Bible, is triune, theological: *Who is God?* (Ontological Trinity) *What is God up to?* (Economic Trinity) Followed by the anthropological: *Don't you want to hitch on to whatever God is up to?*

I was Associate Minister (lackey stuck with youth ministry and running errands for the senior pastor) in a small Southern town. After a rousing rant on how Richard Nixon is ruining America. Or, maybe my theme was, "Follow me! Vanguard of racial justice." Or, "Don't you have a used coat that you can cast to a less fortunate neighbor?" Something prophetic like that.

As I stood at the door after service, craving congregational reaction, pro or contra, Mrs. Bunker emerged, intimidating even though an octogenarian, predatory, under full sail, black hat, gloves, carved headed cane, contemptuous countenance.

"You call that a sermon?" she smirked. "How old are you? Not more than twenty-five, I'd say. Yet you presume to hector from the pulpit? Proffering sophomoric advice as if you were a Methodist Freud? Really now."

Somehow the Holy Spirit implicated herself into Mrs. Bunker's post-sermon devaluation enabling me to say to the Lord, but not to her, "Geeze. The old lady's right."

The sole subject that I had just spent three years in seminary pondering, the one area that I might—even in my callow youth—know more than she, the lone reason for a kid like me insinuating into a life like hers: Talk about God.

My mind changed about preaching. Mrs. Bunker and the Holy Spirit, working the word.

"How can merely mortal me presume to speak for God?" you ask. Truth is, I can't. Only God can speak for God and, wonder of wonders, in preaching, even through your sermons and mine, God condescends to speak.

Karl Barth won the hearts of preachers by calling preaching an "impossible possibility." We can't preach, said Barth, and yet God commands us to preach. No word can be truthfully said about God that doesn't come from God. Yet, the humanly preached word is, by the miraculous grace of God, God's. Thank you, Second Helvetic Confession. Only God speaks for God and, in preachers, God speaks.[2]

I work hard on my sermons, but my scholarly best isn't good enough to preach God's word. Therefore, we do epiclesis, begging the Holy Spirit to help us speak and the church to hear. Trouble is, because the Holy Spirit is one of the three, free, sovereign persons of the one Trinity, the Holy Spirit is under no obligation to show up just because we asked. It's not a sermon until God enters and makes my Southern-accented, frail, elderly voiced words God's word and God is free to show or not.

As Bonhoeffer said, there's only one preacher, Christ. Luther said this one preacher, Christ, uses us preachers on Sunday to equip the whole church to preach God's word to the world the rest of the week.

Your preaching has weaknesses? Take heart. No sermon is so sorry that an incarnating, relentlessly communicative God is unable to utilize your offering, no matter how pitiful. Your preaching, for reasons known only to the Trinity, is a major way God has chosen to love the world.

"You call this a sermon?" the Holy Spirit smirks, peering over your shoulder at your notes. "Give it to me, I'll take it from here."

As I've harped on with seminarians: "We've trained our congregations to expect a sermon to be about them and their alleged problems." Preacher, do you really want to cast yourself as an economist, a self-help guru, a pop psychologist, or a marriage and family expert? Besides, you do well to distrust their self-assessment of their problems.

Why not engage, through your sermon, in a conversation they've been avoiding all week? Talk about the God who, in Jesus Christ, in Scripture, and now in your sermon, wants to talk to us.

About the same time of my assault by Mrs. Bunker ("Now, Miss Edith," I said in response. "That's *Mrs.* Bunker, young man," she bit back), I learned a hermeneutical principle that disciplined my study of Scripture ever since: *Scripture always and everywhere speaks primarily about God and only secondarily and then derivatively about us.*

A sermon is more difficult than a university lecture because preachers have to speak for, to, and from the only God who ever talked to the likes of us.

I'm stuck, with Jesus on a summer's Sunday, at an absurdly affluent, unashamedly all-white church in Long Island. My text? Mark 10:17-31. An upwardly mobile person ("Isn't it nice when someone like you appears in Scripture?" I cackled.) is invited to follow Jesus but declines discipleship. ("Only instance of a refusal of Jesus's invitation. What does that tell you?") Then, leaning toward them, sardonically, "and the reason was money." Brief pause to let that sink in.

"It's hard to save rich people," Jesus comments casually to his disciples once the man is out of earshot.

"How hard is it, Jesus?" they ask.

Jesus replies, "As difficult as to shove a fully loaded camel through the eye of a needle."

"That's hard!" they exclaim.

"Still, with God, anything could be . . . possible," says Jesus, "even the salvation of people who work for Goldman Sachs."

What fun to work with a Savior who doesn't mind throwing the furniture around. The temptation is to make excuses. "He didn't mean, 'Sell all you have and give it to the poor.' That would be economically irresponsible. He meant up your church pledge from the modest Methodist 2.2 percent to a more robust 3.5."

Give 'em the old, "Here's what Jesus would have said if he had the benefit of a Duke Divinity School education."

Be not led into temptation. Your job is to talk about, with, and like Jesus, whether it personally pleases them or you to do so or not.

It's Your Job

Not long ago there was a much-discussed article by a Presbyterian pastor explaining why, after a decade, he was quitting.[3] Worn out by unduly harsh (candid?), politically partisan (Republican) negative lay reaction to his thoughtful (liberal) sermons, he was throwing in the towel. My heart went out to the man, self-pitying preacher that I am. Still, I wanted to say to him, in love, what Bishop Tullis had said to me: *It's your job.*

In 2 Timothy 2:15, Paul refers to Timothy as a fellow *ergaten,* a field hand, a laborer, a "workman." It's a job. That's why I now think of preaching as craft rather than art, a learned set of skills, practices to which we submit. A craft is learned by a novice looking over the shoulder of an experienced craftsperson. (Just what you are doing by reading this book.) *Ergaten* also implies that if one works conscientiously on the craft, you'll get better over time, and that while hearing a sermon may be miraculous, coming up with a sermon requires labor, whether our listeners appreciate it or not. It's not God's word until God makes it so. Yet you, like John the Baptist, prepare the way for the Lord through your endeavor.

"I'm sending you to their hardheaded and hard-hearted descendants, and you will say to them: The Lord God proclaims. Whether they listen or whether they refuse, since they are a household of rebels, they will know that a prophet has been among them" (Ezekiel 2:4-5). Do that in needlepoint, frame it, nail it to the wall of your study, you'll be better for it.

As Paul closes his advice-giving to Timothy, he doesn't tell Timothy to take care of his body, declare a day off, or keep up with the latest theological trends. Instead, Paul says, *pay attention to public reading, preaching, and teaching. Don't neglect the spiritual gift in you that was given through prophecy when the elders laid hands on you. Practice these things, and live by them so that your progress will be visible to all. Focus on working on your own development and on what you teach. If you do this, you will save yourself and those who hear you* (1 Timothy 4:13-16).

I remind you that when the Stranger reached to the fishermen from the shore, calling them, all he promised to do for them was to "teach." And how about the time when Jesus went ashore and encountered a hungry throng and "had compassion on them because they were like sheep without a shepherd. Then he began to teach them many things" (Mark 6:34). Sure, he miraculously fed them, but not before he compassionately taught them.

Called by Jesus, commissioned to speak up and out for Jesus, your chief claim—in slinging Jesus's words into a narcissistic, self-obsessed, "household of rebels"—is not that this sermon will help them make it through the week but that what Jesus says, hard to hear or not, happens to be the truth, and you are the one sent to teach the truth they can't tell themselves.

Telling the Truth

Maybe that's why throughout First and Second Timothy, Paul talks interchangeably about "preaching" and "teaching." As Kierkegaard said, the truth of the gospel doesn't arise from any human heart. Preachers are charged with telling listeners what they don't know until we teach. Listeners are learners who have the challenge of assimilating information (the gospel) that is not common sense, conventional wisdom, or shared human experience.

There will come a time when people will not tolerate sound teaching. They will collect teachers who say what they want to hear because they are self-centered. They will turn their back on the truth and turn to myths. But you must keep control of yourself in all circumstances. Endure suffering, do the work of a preacher of the good news, and carry out your service fully (2 Timothy 4:3-5).

Here Paul sounds as crabby as Tertullian, giving credence to those who suspect that these letters come from a later Paul personifier. Timothy is warned not to accommodate *the truth* to whatever *myths* are marketed at the moment. Unsound teaching is always more enthusiastically received than true because fake gods (idols), having been produced by us, are easier to get along with than the one, true, living (and therefore unmanageable) Trinity who comes to us. Thus, when I was drubbed by a couple of huffy, right wingers after a sermon in a Methodist meeting in Florida, I disobeyed Paul, lost control, and responded to their rebuke with, "Like you, there's much that Jesus says that I find offensive. Sorry, if Jesus makes you uncomfortable but, because of your baptism, listening to Jesus is *your job!*"

If one of your listeners says to you after you've done your job, "Where did you get all of this? I've never heard anything like this," I advise responding, in love, "There are powerful forces to shield you from this un-American message. Where would you have heard this truth? Fox News? In a Duke classroom? Give me a break. No, you had to get dressed and come to church at an inconvenient hour of the week (at least Rotary serves lunch) to hear this."

I know a despairing preacher who quit because, "My people can't tell the difference between a Democrat, a Republican, and a Christian." Though I hate to see him go, he is right to regard as a preaching flop, listeners who confuse the kingdom of God with The American Way Inc.

In my present life as a perennial guest preacher, I can say with authority that there are some words of Jesus that are difficult if not impossible to say if you're not their pastor. What power you have as the one whom they have given permission to talk to them about God. You speak as one who is known preaches to those who are known. Embedded with them (I'm speaking metaphorically, of course), they can't weasel out of what you say (the way they do with me) with, "Well, he's a professor who lives in an Ivory Tower, so what he says is irrelevant to us."

You are located. Contextualized. Context is the major reason why downloading and then preaching sermons directly from my *Pulpit Resource* or worse, from AI, is immoral. You may be weak in Greek, no scholar of Scripture, and not good looking in front of a mic, but one thing you've got going is that you are there, contemporary with your gathered congregation. Their pastor. They have fewer defenses against your sermons than mine.

I'm writing you anonymously. I have a sort of image of you in my mind as I write, but my imagined you is not the real you. And you know next to nothing about me. I therefore must generalize and over-simplify. But when you stand before your people, you don't abstractly speak of "The Racial Problem in America" or "The Economic Plight of the American Family." You see Rachel who has finally, with hours of your pastoral help, summoned the guts to leave her abusive husband. Or the sullen teenager who is trying hard not to listen because he is coerced there by his parents as punishment for wrecking the family car. Then there's Harold who is dying but hasn't told anybody but you. That direct, personal, pastoral relationship makes your sermons better than mine.

And it also accounts for some of your worst preaching.

Reinhold Niebuhr said that before he became a pastor he assumed that there were so many tame, boring sermons because pastors were fearful that, if they said anything challenging, they would be fired.[4] But during his first years as a preacher in a little German-speaking parish in Detroit, Niebuhr realized that preachers trim their messages and deliver safe sermons, not out of fear but rather from love. A pastor learns to love these people mired in their mundane misery. Why make their lives more difficult by reference to the call of Christ?

Still, we preach. We preach because the way you love your people is by telling them the truth about God. Truth trumps empathy. We preach because that's the job we were assigned. We preach because it's so much more interesting to talk about the Trinity than about us. We preach because words are the primary way God connects. We preach because Jesus Christ is just dying to make people's lives more than if they had been left to their own devices. And, to be honest, we preach because it's fun.

"The surgeon thinks she can remove my son's tumor, but my boy may be unable ever to talk or walk again. Your sermon was so helpful." My pitiful homily? Obviously, more was heard than I intended. More occurred than I sought to accomplish. The women running from the tomb on Easter morning told the truth! He's loose. He will have his say.

I'm not sure I would really believe in the active, real, bodily presence of the Third Person of the Trinity were it not for my being made to preach. Every preacher has the experience of doing necessary homework on a sermon, then delivering in a pleasing, engaging, resonant voice with hand gestures from the torso, maintaining eye contact, only to have the sermon fall flat on the floor before the congregation's uncomprehending, Zombie-like stares.

Sermonic flops are everyday, ordinary proof that it takes two to deliver one good sermon. Trouble is, while the Holy Spirit is necessary for a sermon to be a sermon, the Third Person of the Trinity is not obliged to show up just because I begged.

On the other hand, every preacher has the disarming experience of having assembled a few saccharine clichés on the back of an envelope (busy week and a bad cold was my excuse), reassuring the congregation, "Today I'll not trouble you for more than twelve minutes, har, har," only to have someone emerge after service, grip my hand, tears in his eyes, stammering, "That, that was the best sermon you ever preached. I've been living like I shouldn't. I knew I was wrong. But I'll tell you, I'm not the same as I was when you started talking. Thanks."

Staggering back to your study, you say to the Holy Spirit, "I couldn't have done that on my own. Thanks. Maybe."

In honing the craft, my mind has changed more often than in any other area of ministry. I once went back over my earliest sermons and cringed at my puerile, cocky, judgmental, and hackneyed self-display of my exegetical homework. Lecturing a rural Georgia congregation on the deficiencies of Tillich's theology of correlation! Or, "Three Things You Must Do to End Hunger." What was I thinking?

Witness

Preaching is more difficult than most public speaking because preaching is witness, testimony. In a sermon, we either put up or should shut up. When people urge preachers to "preach from the heart," it's their inchoate recognition that preaching is a pastor's declaration of faith. While we are ordained to preach the faith of the church, rather than what's on our hearts, it's fair for listeners to expect congruence between what we believe and what we proclaim.

Of course you have doubts—what preacher doesn't? But the pulpit is not the place to wrestle with your misgivings about the faith delivered by the saints. Paul, as we have seen in his letters to Timothy, did not hesitate to expose himself in his sermons, yet he knew, "We don't preach about ourselves. Instead, we preach about Jesus Christ as Lord, and we describe ourselves as your slaves for Jesus' sake" (2 Corinthians 4:5).

None of Paul's candid self-disclosures match the wallop of Paul's sweeping Christological acclamation: *The mystery of godliness is great: he was revealed as a human, declared righteous by the Spirit, seen by angels, preached throughout the nations, believed in around the world, and taken up in glory* (1 Timothy 3:16).

John Wesley advised his traveling preachers to "preach faith until you have it," implying that preaching is a good way to talk yourself into faith while passing it on to others. (How many of his adamant assertions to Timothy could be chalked up to Paul preaching to himself?)

Hiding in my study five minutes before a funeral for a four-year-old lost to leukemia, I said to the Lord, "I'm not going out there and make some lame excuse for the world you created."

Having been with the family when they got the diagnosis from the doctors, praying for healing every step of the way, I was angry, embarrassed to be the Lord's branch manager.

Somehow the Lord got to me, "It's not about you. Go out there, be obedient to your vocation, and let Paul do the talking. I'd advise Romans 8."

I put on my robe, walked out, read, and preached with gusto Paul's conviction that nothing, even this horror, can separate us from the love of God in Jesus Christ. In telling them what Paul believed, I believed. I pray they did too. If Paul's words aren't true, then they, and I, have nothing to say.

We preachers find our own voice through imitation. Looking back, there was my If-Billy-Graham-had-gone-to-Yale-Divinity-School period. I've also clothed my raspy, Southern-accented voice in the manner of preachers whom I have admired, cross-dressing at various times as Fred Craddock, Walter Brueggemann, Betty Achtemeier, Tom Long, Fleming Rutledge, or Barbara Brown Taylor. Classical student rhetoricians memorized and delivered the speeches of others for a decade before they spoke their own. When John Wesley sent a book with fifty-two of his sermons to his "traveling preachers" he advised, "Preach these sermons before you attempt any of yours."

Still, there will come a time when imitation leads you to confidence in your own voice and you will preach as you preach, not as you have been told to preach.

Take heart that, in preaching, God loves to use your inadequacies and weaknesses. "We have this treasure in clay pots so that the awesome power belongs to God and doesn't come from us" (2 Corinthians 4:7). Every time I preach a passable sermon, God's showing off. "Watch my all-surpassing power use even this cracked pot!"

The pulpit isn't the place to perform a psychological strip-tease. Nobody wants to hear this week's episode of "The Trials and Tribulations of Pastor Bob." It's fine for you to share instances of the actual, personal impact of the gospel on your flawed, finite, incomplete human life. But excessive self-display plays into the hands of an overly self-concerned culture and distracts from the Savior who said that we find ourselves by losing ourselves (Matthew 16:25).

Part of the fun of being a preacher is when you experience God helping you overcome some of your human-all-too-human inadequacies by insisting that you, even with flaws and faults, reservations and timidity, go ahead and preach anyway.

One of my students said that she spent the first twenty years of her life being fed "complementarian" nonsense by her pastor. Whenever she spoke in church, a little voice said, "They don't want to hear you."

Now, after three years of field work at Duke Divinity, the voice says, "Some of them think they don't want to hear me but wait 'till they hear my sermon." Her self-doubts (induced by bad theology) were leveraged by God to make her a most convincing, beguiling spokesperson for the gospel.

I had a student who was charmingly self-effacing, shy, and introverted. Thus, when I first heard him preach, I sat amazed as he came from behind the pulpit, looked us straight in the eye, and insisted on a hearing, God doing amazing things with a life determined to be obedient to God in service to others.

"I was offended by your sermon," said a guy at the church door.

Though I didn't say, I thought, *I don't care.* I marveled that God had taken a dishonest (president of my school classes since the seventh grade, an honor rarely bestowed upon the truthful) flatterer and, by assigning me the job of preaching, had made me relatively truthful. Took the Lord a mere five hundred Sundays to do it.

Karoline Lewis says that many women pastors feel more in charge, self-confident, and free when they preach than in any other ministerial task. In service to the Word, they find themselves attached to and liberated by something that transcends cultural prejudices.

I began as a manuscript preacher who somewhere along the line became a sort of rough outline preacher. Working from a manuscript deluded me into thinking that I was being coherent and clear, controlling the communication. Besides, when you look at your notes, you're not looking at your listeners who are constantly (without even trying) sending clues and cues to help you say your sermon. Which is why online preaching from a studio doesn't quite work.

Then there's the propensity of the Holy Spirit to swoop down, when I'm mid-sentence, rip the sermon out of my hands, romp recklessly through the congregation, and preach a sermon better than the one I had prepared, often accosting people I had no intention to address. Like I said, the Trinity has not given us preachers the power to determine the boundaries of divine/human conversation.

Contributing to the Conversation

When you preach, you make a contribution to the conversation between God and God's people. Then post-sermon, you enjoy where God takes the conversation next week.

Like most pastors, I dread door-to-door visitation of parishioners. Better things to do with my time than wait for them to turn down the TV, come to the door, and expose me to the hound who, "Never bit anyone before. Don't know what he's got against you, preacher."

Yet preparation for preaching forced me into close listening through visitations at home, school, and work. You'll learn more in five minutes in their living room than by greeting them for a decade at the church door. Time and again I've left my study, having despaired over the muteness of next Sunday's appointed lection from Deuteronomy, only to be given revelation in a conversation at someone's kitchen table.

If the laity only knew how dependent we are upon them to make sermons work. And how many times they have unknowingly ruined what could have been an interesting sermon.

Duke University Chapel's urbane, educated congregation broke me of taking as compliment, "That was a wonderfully thought-provoking sermon." I finally figured out what they meant was, "Thinking about God is the way we educated types avoid being obedient to God."

Still, I love that of all the things incarcerated Paul could request, his main ask is for Timothy to *bring the scrolls and especially the parchments* (1 Timothy 4:13). I can list half a dozen instances when I was close to losing faith in my preaching, on the verge of closing up shop. The cure was a book by somebody who had given her life to thinking about God and allowing her to talk me back into the faith, displaying the beauty of sound doctrine and suggesting that I was just the one to share the truth about God with those who have yet to get the news.

When disgruntled retired clergy (a tautology?) attempted to get me booted from my bishopric in Bama, an afternoon brooding with Catherine LaCugna's thick, rich—too rich—book on the economic Trinity enabled me to clinch my fist, grit my teeth, and preach on.[5]

Even my worst days as bishop were redeemed by ending, cloistered in our basement, translating another early sermon by beleaguered young pastor, Karl Barth.[6] You don't have to be a polyglot, voracious reader to survive in ministry—but it helps.

You ask, "How can I keep at ministry over the long haul?" I answer, daily imbibe a bit of Barth.

In my first years, I was desperate to hear others preach, for as I have said, we learn to preach through apprenticeship. Today, you can hear six sermons before breakfast, if you wish, thanks to social media, the contemporary equivalent of Paul's scrolls and parchments. You've got more resources than at any time in the history of the church to show you how (or how not) to preach.

Delivery of a sermon can't be learnt in a seminary homiletics class; engaging sermon presentation is a craft requiring lots of practice. Worry more about the sermon's theological claims than mechanics of delivery. If the message in the bottle is worth discovering, who cares about the condition of the bottle? If the messenger is gripped by a message, the messenger will find a way to deliver it.

Sequestered in a hotel ballroom, listening to a professor drag on about something that interested him, a man rushed to the podium and said, "We have an emergency. Exit quickly, but orderly. I'll show you the way." The announcer didn't need professional training or laborious preparation—nor did we listeners require a personal relationship with him—to win both a hearing and an active response.

Some of my sermonic failures are due to Jesus. It ain't a sermon until he shows up and makes it one. When I complained about the pitiful results of my sermon to an aging but well-heeled church in New York, I think I heard Jesus say on the way out, "Be not so hard on thyself. As you know, I'm uncomfortable in these settings. You did fine, considering what you were up against with that text and this congregation."

Paul lived much of his life comfortably within the boundaries he had set for God's self-communication. Then he was summoned to speak for a Messiah who was determined to be *preached throughout the nations, believed in around the world* (1 Timothy 3:16). Next thing you know, he's in jail.

Yet, we preach. Though there are good reasons why people don't hear and shouldn't even be there on a Sunday, there they are. They're not as biblically knowledgeable as one might like, nor as eager to hear as I had hoped, and God help you if you step on their wacko political prejudices. Still, all over the world, there they are, listening as if their lives depended on it, which of course, they do.

Maybe they haven't gotten word that there's a de-churching "Attendance Recession." Did nobody tell them that Christianity is an outmoded, Jewish, and impractical fantasy that we, living at the summit of human development (Durham, North Carolina) have progressed beyond? Or maybe (and this is more likely) somehow, some way a lavishly revealing Jesus Christ has found a way to kick down their defenses and call to them from the shore, "Follow me."

And guess who gets to play a major role in God's continuing conversation with them?

Preach the word. Be ready to do it whether it is convenient or inconvenient. Correct, confront, and encourage with patience and instruction (2 Timothy 4:2)

Performing the Word

Preaching is judged by its performance in the lives of the saints. The preacher not only speaks from the gospels but also talks like them, acting out the Word on Sundays in church so that the faithful might personify the truth in the world the rest of the week.

May the Lord show mercy to Onesiphorus' household, because he supported me many times and he wasn't ashamed of my imprisonment (2 Timothy 1:16). Paul backs up his authoritative speaking not only by his direct encounter with the risen Christ on Damascus Road but also by naming exemplary members of the Ephesus congregations.

"Let me clarify for you students who are new at the university," I said the first Sunday of the fall term. "Duke Chapel is not the Department of Religious Studies. They sit back and think religion; we enjoy *doing it*. If they were the Department of Sex, *none of us would be here!*"

Another humorless letter from the department chair. Another groveling apology from me.

Visiting an ailing octogenarian congregant as she lay in hospital, I asked for what she would like me to pray.

"Pray that my young doctor will leave me alone. That silly boy intends to subject me to therapy alleged to give me another two years! If I were twenty, I would take up the offer. But why consume resources of those who are younger? It's not 'health care'; it's death denial. No thanks, I've had quite enough."

I left her hospital room muttering, *Baylor was right. I am truly one of the twelve most effective preachers in the English-speaking world.*

Pray, therefore, that each of us will be able to say, when our preaching life is o'er and we've had our last word, *The Lord stood by me and gave me strength, so that the entire message would be preached through me and so all the nations could hear it. I was also rescued from the lion's mouth!* (2 Timothy 4:17).

Matthias Grünewald, *Isenheim Altarpiece,* Colmar, France

Over Karl Barth's desk in Basel is a print of Grünewald's "Crucifixion" from the *Isenheim Altar.* Christian preaching is hard because it must talk about this mystery. Nobody ever, on their own, drifted toward the notion of God Almighty crucified, flayed out like a slaughtered lamb on a cross. Somebody's got to point them toward that inconvenient truth.

Every faithful preacher, said Barth, is a reiteration of John the Baptist. Like John we open the Bible and point to the wonder of a God who allows himself to be driven out of the world on a cross. The best of sermons, said Barth, are but the long boney finger of John the Baptist, gesturing away from ourselves toward Christ.

What a joy to be enlisted to this impossible, utterly necessary role, pointing toward Christ, shouting, "Behold the Lamb of God who takes away the sin of the world!"

> Questions from pastor, speaker, and best-selling author Nadia Bolz-Weber, author of three *New York Times* bestselling memoirs:
>
> 1. Okay, maybe a pastor is not an "expert on a subject," a gleaming example of perfected piety, or a font of biblical information, but isn't a pastor an expert in what it's like to be someone for whom forgiveness of sins is so needed and how the living Word both connects and frees?
>
> 2. Haven't you not only had experience of the terrible mercy of God but also the continual honor of reporting back to God's people about it?

PASTORS ARE MISSION LEADERS

Pastors care for congregations by loving our people and attending them in their times of need. With luck, they'll care for us pastors.

The history of Christian mission shows that mission is tainted by racism, colonialism, and nationalism; take care attempting to share or to enact the gospel with others.

Mission occurs when we who have surplus time and treasure give to those with less.

Now and then, pastors engage in prophetic political action by speaking truth to power, taking leftward stands on social issues and working for a more just American democracy.

"Ministry isn't a mystery, Son," intoned the aging (he was sixty if he was a day), condescending (his predominate posture) preacher in the lobby between sessions at my very first annual conference. "Keep your people happy. Love them, they'll love you. Visit the sick, preach the gospel, but not too much of it. One day, you'll cut your hair and toss your radical ideas. Oh yea, and one more thing, buy property at Junaluska."

"Junaluska?" guffawed I. Methodist mountain Mecca. Two hundred acres without an ashtray or a good drink.

"Name me one man on the bishop's cabinet without a cottage at Junaluska. It's the key to success in this church. Begin with a condo, trade up."

As he hobbled away to hob knob with the more prominent, I prayed, "Lord, strike me dead when I look like that old guy."

You may have similar moments as you read my counsel.

Get this straight: Ministry is not a mutual love affair between pastor and congregation, nor about visiting the sick, offering sage life coaching, or rectifying the moral defects of the flock. The cut of your hair is your business and ideas, radical or not, are beside the point. Ministerial leadership is about hitching on to the mission of Jesus Christ and recruiting others to do likewise.

Maybe it's obvious to somebody as smart as you that First and Second Timothy are missionary propaganda. Mission (Latin, *missio*, sent) is the detonation by Jesus that blows those who know beyond the bounds of the ecclesiastical cognoscenti so that they might show and tell those who don't yet know that Jesus knows them.

Body of Christ in Motion

Whoever said, "Bloom where you are planted," it wasn't Paul. Timothy's ministry is more than fluffing up pillows at church; he's on a wild ride with the restless body of Christ. Paul, inexorably itinerate lead missionary, keeping Timothy on the move, would be clueless about our term "parish pastor":

Do your best to come to me quickly. Demas . . . has deserted me and has gone to Thessalonica. Crescens has gone to Galatia, and Titus has gone to Dalmatia. Only Luke is with me. Get Mark, and bring him with you. . . . I sent Tychicus to Ephesus (2 Timothy 4:9-12).

Paul met Timothy while working out in the multicultural Roman colony of Lystra (Acts 16:1-2). On Paul's first visit, the Lystrians tried worshipping him as a god (poor, credulous fools) then stoned Paul within an inch of his life because he wasn't (Acts 14:6-20). Ah, a day in the life of a missionary.

Timothy's father was a Gentile, his mother Jewish-Christian. Both Timothy's mother and grandmother were brought to baptism by missionary Paul (2 Timothy 1:5; Acts 16:1-2). Timothy remained uncircumcised (2 Timothy 3:15), suggesting that Timothy was part of the shift of Christianity from Asia to Europe as the church made missional adaptations in its move from obscure Jewish sect to major threat to the empire.

The body of Christ in motion, in mission, is who God is. The Father sends the Son, who, in the power of the Holy Spirit, gives his life to the world and sends the world's needs back to the Father so that the one God may be reiterated in the world in three ways. Then the Son calls out to us, "As the Father sent me, so I am sending you" (John 20:21). Trinity, the name of the God who refuses entrapment in divinity, God relentlessly relational, incarnational, creative, and restlessly sending, drawing all into communion with These Three Who Are One.

"When I am lifted up from the earth, I will draw everyone to me" (John 12:32), said magnetic Jesus as announcement of his missional intentions. Mission accounts for why we know next to nothing about Jesus's early life among the good country folk back in Nazareth, as if to say, "Before Jesus sets in motion his mission, what's to know?"

Mission happens whenever the Holy Spirit kicks and drags the church over some human boundary in order to go with God to take the good news of Jesus into all of God's world. The first barrier breached was God's sending of religious terrorist Paul to carry the gospel all the way out to the gentiles, even before they asked. Then Paul was sent to Timothy's mother and grandmother who cast Timothy back to Paul who in turn sent Timothy to establish innovative political enclaves, a.k.a. the churches at Ephesus.

49

Missionary Me

The Lutheran *Augsburg Confession* (1530) defines church as "the congregation of the saints in which the gospel is rightly preached and the sacraments are rightly administered." For Calvin, church is, "Where the Word is heard with reverence and the sacraments are not neglected." Note the introversion in these definitions of church. No mention of mission; we're Christians by being lucky enough to be born in Germany or Geneva. Thus, the church has to keep rediscovering ourselves as missionaries. It's so much easier to huddle at home, keep house, cosseting the saints around the blessed Eucharist, docilely languishing on committees, calling that church.

I took twenty years to understand the first Bible verse I memorized at age six, John 3:16. "God so loved me and people who look a lot like me that God gave . . ." No! "God so loved the world that he gave his only Son . . ." Christ didn't die for the church. He thinks it all belongs to him. If the church won't join Jesus in his mission of reclamation of his world, so much the worse for the church.

Every Christian was made through the work of some missionary. Each congregation was once a new church plant.

I didn't always know this.

One despondent afternoon in the Dog Days of summer, slouching in my study at a flagging little church (not the one I pastored in low-country South Carolina; the later one resting in the up-country), I picked up *Foolishness to the Greeks*. What hath an English bishop, sometime missionary to India, to do with me?

Lesslie Newbigin rearranged my day and the rest of my ministry. By suppertime, Newbigin converted an accommodated, settled, North American, people-pleasing pastoral care prostitute into an emergent missionary. *Foolishness to the Greeks* made my drive home that evening through modern, Western, skeptical, twentieth-century Christendom Greenville a missionary journey through second-century Asia Minor with its cacophony of pagan voices, competing truth claims, and squabbling godlets. In a moment I saw my parishioners, not as standoffish modern skeptics, but as a bunch of credulous pagan fundamentalists and goofy, hot-to-trot, secular fanatics keen to believe anything once given half a chance to believe in something.

Seminary had deceived me into thinking that my job was to make the faith credible to urbane, critically thinking late modern, more-or-less Christian sophisticates—like the people at YDS. Newbigin countered that God wanted me to be a leader of a troublesome missionary enclave going head-to-head with pagans over who tells the truth about God.

I awoke to the Newbiginesque realization that American Christians are missionaries sent into a culture we thought we owned. Duped by the fiction (thank you Reinhold Niebuhr) that America was a more-or-less Christian country, we presumed that we had at last achieved, through the godless Constitution, a society where, for the first time in history, it was safe to be Christian. We were now free to be just as religious as we pleased (if we persisted in this archaic faith) as long as we kept it to ourselves, personal and private (and therefore irrelevant). Jesus Christ is Lord, but that's just my personal opinion.

As a student, I presumed my job was to make South Carolina a bit less racist and the U.S.A. a tad less imperialist. Missiologists like Luke, Newbigin, and Yale's Lamin Sanneh made me a missionary. Turns out, the quarrel between Jesus and the world was greater than frets about the sorry state of Congress. I was given renewed recognition of the perennial abrasion between church and world, the oddness of the gospel, and an invigorating sense that, U.S.A. or U.S.S.R., to hell with common sense.

True, missions got a bad name once we awoke to the realization that Western mission is tainted by sins of race and nation. Not to be defensive about some of the history of "foreign mission," but, growing up in South Carolina, the only way you could receive Christ was from the hands of church basketball coaches, Sunday school teachers, preachers, and janitors (none of whom thought of themselves as missionaries), all of whom were deeply racist and incipiently white nationalist. Somehow

God helped untangle the gospel from this mess so that I could be embraced by a Jesus who was considerably more interesting than the Jesus presented to me by these well-meaning but muddled missionaries.

If you're a heathen who thinks you are too good to meet Christ through an often misinformed, malformed Christian missionary, I'm not sure how you plan to get to know the fully human/fully divine Christ. The checkered history of mission is an affirmation not only that Christ saves sinners but also surprisingly saves sinners by using sinners to convince fellow sinners that Christ saves sinners, only sinners.

Mission Leader

Mission doesn't happen without someone stepping up and taking responsibility for being the leader who helps us get in step with Jesus. I've not known a congregation to decline for reasons other than their refusal to be sent and a pastor who lacks the skill to argue them into and to organize them for mission. All turnarounds of dwindling churches begin when someone has the guts to ask three missional questions: *What portion of his mission has Christ assigned to us? Who in this congregation is already participating in that mission? How can we undergird them and recruit more of the baptized to join them in mission?*

As pastor you're to equip God's people for ministry, not take away their baptismally bestowed vocation as missionaries. You're the Mission Leader, not the Professional Missionary upon whom the faithful have dumped their baptismal responsibility. Nor are you the Surrogate Social Activist, busy doing political agitation on behalf of the congregation because you don't have the leadership competencies to equip the baptized to be missionaries. Before asking, "How can I meet this need?" always ask, "Who in this congregation is God already calling to meet this need?"

You will know that you are an able mission leader when you ask for "prayer requests" on Sunday and somebody seeks prayer for a need more pressing than the physical deterioration of older adults quartered within your congregation.

"You walked off a good paying job and went back to school in Social Work?" I asked her, incredulously shouting into the phone. No wonder your parents are furious. Duke education down the drain. And you pushing thirty. What possessed you?

"Oh, I see. Hmm. . . . Something *I* said back in that dormitory Bible study on Romans? I see. Yes. . . . Well, er, uh, you and Jesus have a good time. Bye."

Hastily ending that uncomfortable conversation, I thought to myself, or maybe the Lord said to me, "Look at you. By the grace of God, missionary recruiter after all."

Behind First and Second Timothy is the shock: "Has God's salvation gone even to the Gentiles?" (see Acts 11:18). Faithful churches reach out and grow in order to keep close to a barrier-breaking, peripatetic, imperialistic, universalist, salvation-for-all Savior. My own denomination is rapidly declining, not due to the wreckage wrought by a bunch of yahoo "traditionalist" disaffiliates from Texas, or a minority of self-righteous, ideological, virtue signaling, trendier-than-thou "progressives" in Illinois, but because North Carolina Methodists limited the scope of the church to the one generation (mine) with whom pastors felt most comfortable keeping house. Look at our numbers. Jesus is not nice to churches who refuse to be sent.

"So I quit my job as a stockbroker, anybody can make a lot of money in the market, in order to be a full-time 'house Dad,'" he explained. "We're going to rescue three kids who want to be Christians if it's the last thing we do."

I know a pastor who thought he had nailed down the "biblical view" on same-sex love, singing, "It's a no, no, this I know, for the Bible tells me so." Trouble was, his congregation began a ministry (mission) to a nearby community college. Meals, transportation, Bible study, counseling, alcohol-free parties. Wonder of wonders, the students, underserved by poor support systems on campus, responded.

"In six months we were in regular, close contact with a hundred students!" exclaimed the accidental missionary. "Turns out, we were better evangelists than we thought. We met many who didn't fit our simple, 'You're one or the other,' definitions of Christian young adults. How should we respond to their, 'But what about us?'"

Subsequent congregational discussion and prayer led to an evangelism-induced revision of the pastor's (and the congregation's) attitudes about queer inclusion in the life of the church.

"Those young Christians moved me from 'either/or' to 'both/and,'" testified the pastor. Don't risk mission if you are squeamish about working with the salvific reach of the long arm of Jesus who invites all to his font and table.

Missionary Prayer

In the church today, prayer is mainly therapeutic. For Paul, it was an aspect of mission. Rather than tell Timothy to pray for the wounded within the congregation Paul tells him to make the Ephesians *Pray for kings and everyone who is in authority* (1 Timothy 2:2). Paul mentions Timothy's recurring illness, but doesn't tell him to pray for healing, recommending a swig of wine rather than supplication (1 Timothy 5:23), perhaps because Paul got "no" in response to his repeated prayers for healing of his mysterious "thorn in the flesh" (2 Corinthians 12:7). Paul thought the point of prayer is more than merely medical.

Pray for kings and everyone who is in authority [who often make our lives so miserable], *so that we can live a quiet and peaceful life in complete godliness and dignity* (1 Timothy 2:2). Why pray for the bigwigs who run Hamas, Israel, Russia, Ukraine, Congo, and the USA? Because God *wants all people to be saved and to come to a knowledge of the truth* (1 Timothy 2:4). All. It isn't like they've got their gods and we've got ours, *There is one God and one mediator between God and humanity, the human Christ Jesus, who gave himself as a payment to set all people free* (1 Timothy 2:5-6). And guess whom the one God has appointed to hand over that news to all? *I was appointed to be a preacher and apostle of this testimony—I'm telling the truth and I'm not lying! I'm a teacher of the Gentiles in faith and truth* (1 Timothy 2:7).

The Romans prayed to the emperor. Paul enjoins Timothy to pray for the emperor. I detect no reverence for the government here. About the best you can say for the emperor is that he provided good roads for peripatetic missionary Paul. Before he threw him in jail.

I ask that requests, prayers, petitions, and thanksgiving be made for all people. Pray for kings and everyone who is in authority so that [these pagans in high places will leave us alone and] *we can live a quiet and peaceful life in complete godliness and dignity* (1 Timothy 2:1-2).

If I had been Paul I would have pled, "Pray that the emperor will let me out of jail!" Paul could have forbidden Timothy to pray for the pagan emperor, or urged him to obey the emperor, to resist the emperor, to kill the emperor, to win points by serving in the emperor's army and killing for the emperor, or heroically to sacrifice himself as a martyr at the hands of the emperor. Instead, Paul pled for prayers for the emperor.

Emperors come and go, good and bad. But make no mistake, there are always emperors. It is not a matter of if we will serve somebody but whom we will serve. These days, we don't worry much about the emperor because the emperor who imprisons us is us, our own egos, most imperious of masters.

I began ministry in the heady days of the late Sixties, confident that the church could be a team player with those who work for political change in American society, thinking Jesus's command to love unrealistic (thanks again, Niebuhr), and instead working for justice. Although we've been frustrated by our inability to overcome personal sin in a bedroom, we can wipe out social, systemic sin if we just get the right people in Congress. Why stop with stamping out adultery, let's save the planet. Look at the huge impact we church types made on Civil Rights and Vietnam. Couldn't have done it without us. Right?

Eventually, I became less confident that Christian "social action," as we called it—lobbying Congress, passing righteous laws to force our political vision on others, attempting to make the USA a tad more just, a bit less violent—was the major mission of the church.

When the religious right discovered that two can play at the game of legislative coercion, I began to sense that we Christians, in order to be in the room with the politically powerful, had given away the store (Christologically speaking). We trimmed down Christ's eschatological vision and radical politics to that which could be democratically achieved. "Christian realism" (Niebuhr, hard habit to break), Jesus's imperative, "Follow me!" watered down to, "Get out the vote!"

You argue that whereas Paul and Timothy lived in an autocracy where they could have no impact on the emperor's antics, we are fortunate to live in a democracy. Trouble is, politics is not only the major means of organizing our collective hatreds and resentments, it's also our chief God-substitute. We the people are now king. It's up to you to make the world turn out right by the means of the world. With this kind of foolishness abroad, you get the Institute on Religion and Democracy (IRD). Christian nationalism lite.

True, as bishop I joined the Episcopal and Catholic bishoprics to sue the governor and legislature of Alabama over their draconian immigration laws. (We won!) And I led my congregation to Moral Mondays demonstrations in Raleigh.

Still I say, get real about the limits of legislative political activism. If you were one of the minority of Americans who voted in the last national election, I worry if you felt personal potency when you pulled that lever. Maybe voting encourages the emperor's pretentions. Does your activism and "prophetic" sermonizing imply to your people that politics is the only effective means of doing justice and that the secular state is the functional equivalent of the kingdom of God?

Go ahead and be politically active, if that's what God calls you to do and you are good at it, but be careful; you work within a national polity where many can't tell the difference between a Christian and an American, where the democratic state claims to be the only deity worthy of the sacrifice of our children, sole source of justice, security, and peace.

Though maybe you can move the needle toward a godlier polity in the next election, can you influence world events? It would have been easier if Paul had said, "Work for peace with justice." He said, *Pray for kings and everyone who is in authority,* scurrilous though they may be. The pompous clowns are in God's hands, whether they know it or not. Pray for mercy.

Seems like forever since I prayed in public for the souls of Hamas; how about you?

What is realistically within the realm of your political power is to pray to and partner with God in creating an outpost of the kingdom of heaven: your congregation.

God thinks nations are a joke (Psalm 2:4). God's strategy for establishing justice, security, and peace isn't the emperor, democratically elected or not; God's good idea is your church. Though I might not have chosen to rescue the world in this way, your church does appear to be Christ's way.

Pray for kings and everyone who is in authority. Even rotting in the emperor's jail, Paul obeys Christ's command to pray for our persecutors (Matthew 5:44; Luke 6:28).

Elsewhere, Paul says that he believes that governing authorities owe their authority to God (though they are oblivious), implying that God will hold them to stricter standards than those of us to whom such power has not been bestowed (Romans 13). Pray that God won't hold their records against them. And pray that God won't punish us for our collaboration with their nationalistic delusions.

All that is to argue that the most political thing we can do is to be the church, to do the hard congregational work that's required to be a people who look different than the world. The emperor wields worldly power and basks in godless glory. The church obeys incarcerated, crucified Jesus, prays for all, even those who have contempt for the church, and thereby shows the world the possibility of a people of peace in a world at war.

Jesus forever made prayer problematic by teaching us to pray politically, "Bring on your kingdom!" (Matthew 6:10), even ordering prayer for enemies (Matthew 5:44). There's no way we would pray like that without coercion from Jesus, backed up by a congregation whose prodding and support make prayer in Jesus's name possible even for enemy haters like us.

As Stanley Hauerwas and I put it, when the church is asked, "Say something that's politically effective," we say, "church." The world finds this bewildering. But isn't it comforting to know that those pastor/preacher/leader things you do to foster Christian community in a world of competing, self-interested, rugged individualists are politics, Jesus style?

The hour you spent visiting the nursing home resident after her stroke, you, her only visitor, was, in its way, an act of clinch-fisted resistance against the powers-that-be.

See the Stranger, reaching from the Galilean shore to the fishermen, assembling, then squatting together in the dust, saying, "The revolution begins, here, now. You—yes you, even you, all of you—go into the world, all of it, and announce the threat of God's regime change, catching people, signing them up for rebellion. Caesar, Almighty Death, dethroned. Like it or not, here comes the kingdom of heaven!"

An absurd claim to an absurdly inadequate troupe—unless the Stranger who calls, convenes, commissions, and sends happens to be the Son of God.

Salvation for All

Paul doesn't refer to himself as "Senior Pastor"; he's *teacher of the Gentiles* (1 Timothy 2:7). *I ask that requests, prayers, petitions, and thanksgiving be made for all people* (1 Timothy 1:1) is the first thing that Paul tells Timothy in his first letter (1 Timothy 2:1). The first business of church? Prayer for *all people,* in church or out. *All?* This universal reach is not because pagans (at least the more humane among them) can be nice people too, once you learn to appreciate them for who they are. We pray for *all* because *God . . . wants all people to be saved and to come to a knowledge of the truth.* All. On the cross, *Christ set all people free,* without qualification. It's our joyful task to give that *testimony* to all.

Servants in the church should be dignified, not two-faced, heavy drinkers, or greedy for money. They should hold on to the faith . . . be dignified and not gossip . . . sober and faithful in everything . . . faithful to their spouse and manage their children and their own households well (1 Timothy 3:8-9, 11-13).

I'd guess I'm batting maybe three out of Paul's twelve. Thank God that God's not done with this servant of the church. By God's grace, I, even I, may become *dignified and not gossip* before my last roundup.

When Jesus sends out the Seventy, he assigns them the same work that he does: "Whenever you enter a town and its people welcome you, eat what is set before you [yes, even Myrtle Brown's carcinogenic Red Velvet Cake]; cure the sick who are there [don't give up on the alcoholics], and say to them, 'God's kingdom has come upon you.' [so all will know they're included]" (Luke 10:9).

These seventy missionaries report back to the boss exclaiming, "Lord, even the demons submit to us in your name" (Luke 10:17). A perquisite of pastoral ministry is a front row seat on Christ's grand retake of his world through the ministrations of ordinary saints. Don't miss the show.

Some pastors are exhausted, not because it's hard work but because the work they're doing is inconsequential to Christ's mission. You're supposed to be bored, tired, and burned out if, 1. You try to be the sole missionary, and 2. You reduce leadership to keeping house among the faithful few rather than getting out and about in the unfolding pageant of the *Missio Dei.*

"This congregation loves one another. We're like a family. When any member has a need, we've got their back."

Sorry, that's not good enough for Jesus.

God promises through the *Missio Dei* to reclaim the world, with or without our help. Loving, congregational pastoral care is insufficient; faithful Christian leadership can never be merely parochial and ought not degenerate into feeding people's already obsessive self-concern. Any congregation that is little more than a warm-hearted club, a church that's not actively, daringly following Christ across cultural, racial, ideological, national boundaries (mission), surprised by whom Christ drags in the door, is unfaithful to his politically charged, "Follow me."

"You didn't choose me, but I chose you and appointed you *so that you could go and produce fruit*" (John 15:16, italics mine).

I confess that in my first days of ministry, I did mostly internal congregational maintenance, presenting myself as the most available, loving pastor ever, certainly better than my sluggardly predecessor. Why? Because an unctuous pastoral care giver, 1. Requires no theological training, and 2. Is rewarded by church folks who are always grateful for pastors who make them and their personal needs the point of church.

Soothing ruffled feathers of the faithful, easy; risking a reach to someone outside the circle of the saints, hard. Identifying those who agree with you, easy. Converting those who are confused about God, hard. Caucusing with folk who think just like you, easy; herding the hissing, scratching cats whom Christ has assembled in your congregation (without consulting you), hard. Running errands for families in my church is easier than asking, "Anybody know someone in our neighborhood who could be blessed by this church?"

"Let's be sure to honor those dear saints who have been faithful to this congregation," easy. Daring to ask, "What might give this beloved congregation a future?" Hard.

Greeting prospective members with, "I'll introduce you to some of our nice folks who are just like you," blurs the line between church and country club. Missionary evangelists say to prospects, "We need you to help us be a more faithful congregation and here's how we can help you be more faithful to your baptismal vocation."

"Salvation for all!" was the anti-Calvinist battle cry of John Wesley's Methodist circuit riders. Christ saves the church from itself by recruiting and equipping it to participate in his salvation of all. The day is over, if it ever were, when it was enough to say, "Come to us; great music, a plethora of programs, drug-free kids, inspirational preaching. Doors open at 10:30 am." The so-called attraction model ("You are welcome to come to us.") is running out of steam. Now we're called to be extroverted, evangelistic missionaries. "We'll come to you." *Inclusion* isn't a strong enough term for what Christians are compelled by Christ to offer. We do resourceful, active seeking, searching, followed by gracious welcome.

I remind you that, though they were as ignorant as could be, the only thing the Stranger, reaching to the first disciples, promised to teach was how to "fish for people." Everything else that Jesus teaches is subsequent and subservient to people catching.

I've never seen a congregation move from being centripetal, introverted, and self-concerned to centrifugal, extroverted, and evangelistic without somebody (like you?) stepping up and taking responsibility to lead mission. No congregation exceeds their pastor's vision. The good news is that, for reasons known only to God, God tapped you for this demanding, risky, stressful, invigorating, life-giving work. What if God had passed you over for Lead Missionary and called you instead to be a U.S. Senator?

Somebody must do all those mundane duties required to keep up with the risen Christ. Pastors work for the creation of a reasonably united, invigorated congregation because such congregations are most effective in mission. With a critical eye we watch over Sunday worship so that it's biblical, rich, and inspiring because that's what missionaries need in order to sustain their difficult work in a world that is God's yet is so well organized against God. We pastorally care for the sick in body, mind, and soul in order to bandage them up and send them back to the front lines of Christ's invasion.

Keep ever before you the conviction that God elects the church to embody God's gracious intent beyond the bounds of the church. Others may be enemies of our country, or adversaries of the American way; God is not their enemy. If the church condemns the lifestyle of a group of people, the sinfulness of another culture, or the foreign policy of some hostile nation, we are under divine compulsion to make clear that God has elected them to be our sisters and brothers by electing *all* for God's salvation (1 Timothy 2:3-4). Mercy trumps condemnation when the church turns from talking about Jesus to talk with fellow sinners about sin in the name of a Savior who saves only sinners. How? Through the missionary endeavor of sinners partnering with God in saving fellow sinners.

Paul tells Timothy that he's a missionary because of the God we've got. *God is the one who saved and called us with a holy calling* (2 Timothy 1:9). Not only did God save us, God "called us." Theological damage was done when salvation was disconnected from vocation, turning salvation into individual soul destiny, implying that salvation (our relationship to God) is an individual possession, a membership privilege rather than an evangelistic assignment. *This wasn't based on what we have done, but it was based on his own purpose and grace* (2 Timothy 1:9). And what was God's gracious "purpose and grace"? *God our savior, who wants all people to be saved and to come to a knowledge of the truth* (1 Timothy 2:3-4).

Mission and Conflict

My theory is that there is unproductive conflict and trivial quarreling in many congregations because they talk only to themselves. Boredom (and an uneasy sense that church is meant to be more than this cozy club) breeds congregational contentiousness. The conflict that validates a church as Christ's is not that of squabbling, miffed church members but the tension provoked by the church colliding with the world's resistance to Christ's reign.

In *Leading with the Sermon* I recounted one of my first experiences of moving from being a care-giving pastor to an extroverted Lead Missionary:

> "You need to thank Preacher Baker for what he's done for you here," said Trinity's lay leader, the indomitable Peggy Hursey, as she welcomed me as pastor.
>
> "How would you characterize George's leadership?" I asked Peggy.
>
> "George told six or seven malcontents to go to hell. No preacher had been man enough to tell 'em where to get off. Now this church is ready to rock and roll," she replied.
>
> As he gathered his books, George had advised, "Do scales on the piano first thing on Sundays before you preach. With your scratchy voice, you need that. Keep your tempo up in a sermon; energy in the pulpit is contagious. God knows this crowd needs energizing. One more thing, son: they love to fight. Bunch of Barbarians. Keep 'em fighting the Devil or they'll turn and kill you!"
>
> "How do I do that?" I asked in a trembling voice.
>
> "Find out where Satan is in this town, tell 'em about it, then turn 'em loose."
>
> In less than two months, after a group of United Methodist women observed police brutality at the local jail, with help from Micah, I preached a sermon about the evils of corrupt law enforcement, citing our Lord as a noteworthy victim.
>
> Fighting back tears I said, "Two of our saints, Eleanor and Mary, this week engaging in their ministry at the jail, observed a policeman roughing up a young man in a back cell. When they complained to the chief, he actually said to these two missionaries that . . ." (eyes filled with tears, hardly able to speak). " 'You church ladies look after your church stuff and I'll look after my jail.' "
>
> Congregational gasp. Someone on the third pew shouts, "Busby's got two boats and an Eldorado on a cop's salary?"

"And a riding lawnmower!" added another.

I fully expected them to begin furiously tossing *Methodist Hymnals.*

"Now I can't speak for you," I continued, barely regaining my composure, "but I for one find it hard to sit back and let our dear church, and these dear women, be insulted by a questionable cop."

During the pandemonium I gave an altar call for anyone Jesus had summoned to work against cops gone bad and turned 'em loose. Helping Hand ministry was born. The chief was out of office six months later.[1]

Body of Christ in motion in mission.

Timothy 1 and 2 remind us that Paul didn't know how to create a missional congregation that's both faithful and peaceful. Why should we? Does Paul teach Timothy to avoid conflict, pour oil on troubled waters, practice non-anxious leadership, be gracious and reconciling, listen and don't judge, patiently look for the uncontested middle, or any of the other slogans by which pastors protect themselves from having conflicted conversations on painful subjects?

On the contrary, Paul prods young Timothy to dive in, confront, argue, contest, and turn up the heat:

Preach the word. Be ready to do it whether it is convenient or inconvenient. Correct, confront, and encourage with patience and instruction. There will come a time when people will not tolerate sound teaching. They will collect teachers who say what they want to hear. . . . They will turn their back on the truth and turn to myths. But you must keep control of yourself in all circumstances. Endure suffering, do the work of a preacher of the good news, and carry out your service fully (2 Timothy 4:2-5).

Jesus never walked away from an argument; indeed, he initiated most of them. Judging from First and Second Timothy, and the entire New Testament, there's never been a faithful church free of rancor, debate, and sometimes acrimonious, dangerous division.

The source of good church conflict? A crucified Savior and the *Missio Dei* into which he casts us. Our main task is not the avoidance of pain, or the quelling of all disagreement; our task is participation in the mission of Christ and engagement with conflict that comes with the world's resistance to the gospel *whether it is convenient or inconvenient*. Don't believe me? Read South Bronx Pastor Heidi Neumark's wonderful *Breathing Space*.[2]

Critics have noted that the history of Christian mission is ambiguous at best, sad commentary on the sin of the church at its worst. Christian mission, particularly that led by the Western Church in the last two centuries, has been justly charged with imperialism as the romantic lure of "foreign missions" mingled with hatred of Islam, colonialism, racism, and assertion of cultural superiority.

And yet, Christian missionaries translated the Scriptures, not only into other languages, but into vernacular, idiomatic speech, saving countless indigenous languages, and learning the everyday speech of those they hoped to evangelize. The New Testament was written in *koine*, Greek of the people. Learning another's vernacular dialect is a most humbling, affirming, submissive, and loving gift. Think about that as you call on members of the congregation asking, "What's it like to be a hog farmer these days? I need to know how you talk Monday through Friday so that I can be comprehended when I proclaim Jesus on Sunday."

Christian mission is no longer dominated by the West; mission is everyone going everywhere. More Muslims are becoming Christian than at any other time in history. No one can accurately count the number of churches springing up in China with a government that thinks it prohibits the founding of churches. Over seventy years of state-enforced atheism succeeded only in making the former Soviet Union one of the most surprising mission opportunities. Korean congregations are about the most exciting thing happening in The UMC as those to whom the gospel was given a century ago teach us how to do church in ways we forgot.

On my way to lead worship at a dwindling downtown congregation (a tautology?), I drove by no less than thirteen congregations, six of whom were birthed in the last decade. "What does that tell you?"

asked the Lord with a grin as I unlocked the door to a vast, mostly empty church building with twenty exterior doors, all but one of which is locked all week.

Sending of the Apostles, Vézelay

One Sunday afternoon we trekked to one of France's great Romanesque masterpieces, Vézelay Abbey. Just over the front door, welcoming pilgrims, is a stirring depiction of Christian mission, the tympanum sculpture, *Sending of the Apostles.* Christ almost tumbles from his throne, hands outspread, robes fluttering in fierce Pentecostal wind, as he thrusts his apostles to the four corners of the earth in mission.

Who but the church would welcome people at the front door with an image of the Holy Spirit scattering the church? Welcome to church where shortly you will be shoved out of church in mission.

Just a few feet from the front door of the Abbey, on a hill overlooking the countryside, a simple iron cross marks where, in 1146, Saint Bernard, in a rip-roaring sermon, whipped up the Second Crusade, sending thousands to the Holy Land to kill Muslims in the name of the Prince of Peace.

It's a reminder that we missionaries work under both divine commission and judgment. Christ uses sinners—who, in our evangelism and mission, sinfully warp and distort his good news—to take the good news to sinners that Jesus Christ saves sinners, only sinners, using the missionary efforts of sinners.

When the church has, time and again, screwed up by presuming a status with God that others don't have, we've been judged. Whenever we've used the world's means to convert the world such as a crusade or PR campaign, we've been disciplined. When we've kept the good news to ourselves as if it's ours, we've been humbled by having to rehear the word of God spoken to us by those of whom we don't approve. (Is the tacky, Jesus Jamboree, Independent Megachurch outside of town God's judgment on my staid, middle-of-the-road Methodism?)

No culture, government, or lousy parenting, no university curriculum, no matter how godless and Jesus resistant, has successfully kept this truth from being spoken and enacted. No preacher, no matter how cowardly, inept, or poorly endowed, has restrained God from having God's say to God's world, brashly talking to whomever God pleases. Preachers, take heart! The good news about Jesus, though constantly contested, shall, at the last, by God's grace, fill the earth as the waters cover the sea (Habakkuk 2:14).

God *wants all people to be saved and to come to a knowledge of the truth* (1 Timothy 2:4).

Questions from William J. Barber, II and Jonathan Wilson-Hartgrove, pastors, justice advocates, and authors, Center for Public Theology and Public Policy at Yale Divinity School.

1. Despite all the ways Christian mission has been tainted by racism, colonialism, nationalism, and greed, you celebrate that sinners have still preached the good news to sinners—that you yourself received the gospel from people entangled in the South's distorted version of Jesus that we've called "slaveholder religion." From your own experience of disentangling the gospel from harmful religion, reflect on what a missional church can offer people who've experienced religious trauma and Christian nationalism.

2. [When congregations be satisfied with offering their] members the amenities of a social club, you challenge pastors to point outward to God's mission beyond the church walls. What does Jesus demand of us when we try to do good in our communities? And how does Jesus challenge congregations to re-imagine the "we" of a missional community?

3. You've noted that public ministry has often been individual clergy lining up for causes liberal or conservative. The basic gospel distinction, you note, isn't between liberals or traditionalists, Democrats or Republicans, but the church and the world. But we've seen pastors use this framing to retreat from public ministry. In our experience, there is no way to preach good news to the poor in America today without joining poor and low-income people in building a movement to challenge a death-dealing economy. We know that you and your flock have shown up for Moral Mondays. How does this sort of public ministry fit into your vision of a missional community?

EVANGELISTS, ALL

> It's arrogant for Christians to believe that we possess the truth, therefore evangelism and mission are suspect.

In the spring of 1739 George Whitefield wrote John Wesley that the crowds coming to hear him preach were so large that he needed Wesley's help. Proper Oxford don Wesley recoiled at the unorthodox idea of preaching to the masses in the fields. But the next Sunday, while preaching on the Sermon on the Mount, it occurred to Wesley that Jesus delivered his greatest sermon in a field, even though surely many synagogues were available. "I thought saving souls a sin if not in a church," he reflected.[1] Wesley joined Whitefield in extroverted activity, preaching anywhere people would lend their ears. Welcome to the Wesleyan revival.

Rather than shocking unbaptized Americans with the good news, we Protestant mainliners baptized American culture, transforming the gospel into a message nine out of ten Americans already believed. Gospel rendered into a technique for making nice people even nicer. Force God to be vague, spiritual and helpful, nonjudgmental, undemanding and affirming: Surprise! Everybody believes in God. Why bother with baptism?

Rembrandt, *Christ Preaching*, called *La Petite Tombe*, 1657

Middle-of-the-road, moderate to the point of mediocrity, Methodists like me don't know how to be odd. Most of the theology I imbibed in seminary was in the accommodation mode. It took the burgeoning literature on the missional church to impress me with the faith's weirdness. One thing the gospel is not is common sense that Americans are born believing. The expansive, cosmic, boundary-breaking gospel refuses to respect the limits of attenuated, constricted, modern imagination. Jesus's wild claims are imperialistic and can't be made safely personal; he thinks it all belongs to him. Jesus shall reign and he doesn't care who knows it.

Midway in ministry, I was asked to do a commentary on Acts. I prepared by making my own translation of the Acts of the Apostles (take that, Paul Minear who smacked me with a B- in Greek at YDS). Translation not only forced me to pay attention to the text but also immersed me in Luke's utterly extroverted missionary mindset: Hold on to your hats as the gospel is taken by the Holy Spirit from Jerusalem, Judea, Samaria "to the end of the earth," otherwise known as Greenville, South Carolina (Acts 1:8).[2]

Resident Aliens

From the afternoon of my encounter with Newbigin in Greenville it was inevitable that I would fall into the waiting arms of Stanley Hauerwas in Durham, beginning one of the great theological friendships and accelerating my intellectual development. Let us be a lesson: Nobody becomes Christian on their own and nobody grows closer to Christ solo. Jesus is too demanding to follow without help from his friends.

Do your best to come to me quickly. Demas . . . has deserted me and has gone to Thessalonica. Crescens has gone to Galatia, and Titus has gone to Dalmatia. Only Luke is with me. Get Mark, and bring him with you. . . . I sent Tychicus to Ephesus (2 Timothy 4:9-12).

Stanley clarified my notion of my congregation as a mission outpost and late twentieth-century America as the toughest mission field we've ever tried to crack. He taught me how to unashamedly talk Christian and to teach that weird, unnatural speech to others, helping people to rename their lives and the world with a Jew from Nazareth who was born embarrassingly, lived briefly, died violently, rose unexpectedly, returned to the same losers who forsook him, *and* sent them out as evangelists to tell all the truth about God.

Resident Aliens was the most notable fruit of friendship with Stanley. Amid the astounding readership of that little book, people asked about sources. "Anabaptists?" While I wrote my senior thesis at Wofford on "The Anabaptist View of the Church," I never met a Mennonite until Stanley showed me one. No, my construal of the church as resident aliens is indebted to the Black church in South Carolina, a people saving their children from the slings and arrows of a white supremacist culture.

I was also encouraged in my resident aliens inclination when God displaced me from Greenville urban ministry to university chaplaincy at Duke. First, they entitled me "Minister to the University" (though few on campus viewed me as their minister), then "Chaplain" (Terry

Sanford, upon hiring me, quipped, "Back when I was gov'na of the Nort Ca'lina, I appointed chapl'ins to insane asylums and prisons. How come Duke needs one?"). Eventually they made me "Dean of the Chapel," sequestering me in Neogothic grandeur. It was whispered that one Duke president referred to me as Clerical Pain in the Ass.

The Lord had a different title in mind, anointing me Lead Missionary/Evangelist. "Don't let the university administration know you work for me," Jesus advised. "They might take it the wrong way."

When a student asked, "How could Dean Willimon improve his preaching?" Hauerwas replied, "He's charming. Terminally. I would like to see him preach so obviously that the president would exclaim, 'We're paying the salary of a guy who's preaching against everything we believe?'"

Like Paul, I can't tell the difference between "missionary" and "evangelist." Evangelists hand over the good news that God is not who nine out of ten Americans thought God was. Missionaries, in word and deed, demonstration and improvisation, take the good news about God over some humanly imposed boundary. Though I told nobody, I aspired to be Kierkegaard reintroducing Christianity to Danes who, inoculated with a touch of Christian virus, thought themselves immune to the real thing. Or Flannery O'Connor who said her work depicted "the action of grace in territory held largely by the devil."[3]

In twenty years as "Dean of the Chapel," I discovered that Newbigin and Paul were right; when it comes to reckoning with a crucified God, there are basically two types, Jews and Greeks. The gospel is nuts to credulous Gentiles, trips up Bible-loving Jews (1 Corinthians 1:23). At YDS I had been trained to think that my job was to lessen the gap between Jesus and modern, thoughtful people who drive Volvos. Now I saw my task as widening the gap, pointing to the distance between our notions of "God" and the Son of God.

As undercover evangelist, there were wonderful moments when I was blindsided by Jesus sabotaging enemy defenses, recapturing occupied territory, reminding me that no preacher works solo.

A couple of guys implored me to be on the board of their fraternity as a way to win points with the dean. (Poor schmucks. The dean, a lapsed Episcopalian, despised me.) Palm Sunday afternoon I was summoned to an emergency meeting of the trustees of the frat.

Palm Sunday!

"So," began the ex-Anglican, contemptuously, "tell us what happened at the party on Friday."

"Look, I didn't know the SAE was standing behind me when I tried to slug the KA who was hitting on my date. My elbow came back, that guy's nose was in the wrong place, wrong time. It was unfortunate . . ."

"The person passed out in the stairwell? Er, uh we poured powder on him because one of our dates complained that he was stinking . . ." So went the interrogation.

I blurted, "That's it! I resign from this stupid board. I've better things to do. This will come as a surprise to you philistines; today is Palm Sunday. One of the biggest days of the church year. I've preached two services this morning and have six more this week. I'm out of here."

As I stamped forth with all the righteous indignation I could muster, this unshaven frat boy, leaning against the door burbled, "Nailed it this morning."

"What?"

"One of your greatest hits," he continued. "What's new to be said on lame Palm Sunday? Right? But you? Lex liked your temptation sermon, First Sunday of Lent. But, today, well, you nailed it."

"*You* come to services in the chapel?" I asked.

"Almost every Sunday. Regretted that promise the moment I made it to God. And what kind of pastor doesn't even know who listens to him preach?" rolling his eyes.

"Er, uh, here's my card. You and I have business. Let's do lunch."

As I slithered into my sensible Subaru to scurry back to the safety of suburbia, I said sullenly, "You did that, didn't you? To make me look bad!"

The Lord replied, "Let's go over this one more time. I didn't die for the church. The whole world is mine. I will save those whom I save. Now that you've dropped off that frat board, you and your pious pals have a good time playing church at the chapel."

Jesus!

Go, Show, Tell!

Tertullian said in a sermon that God's people come, not from a woman's loins, but from conversion in the baptismal font. (Promise never to preach that line, even if a saint said it.) Paul could be blasé about marriage and critical of the rich because this kingdom grows not by children through coitus but rather by conversion. (Careful how you put that in a sermon.) Salvation is more than a matter of individual soul-destiny and personal decision; it's by God's choice of some, even the rich, to live uniquely on behalf of others who do not yet know that they, too, have been chosen. We're not only here to be blessed but to bear Christ's blessing to others. The mission is fishin'.

The resurrected Christ does not say, "I have been raised from the dead; now you will see your loved ones when you die," though that may be implied. The Easter word is the angel's evangelical missionary mandate, "Go! Tell!" (see Mark 16:7).

We are commanded to go preach because, while the gospel is more than words, it is never less than words and this word cannot be spoken to ourselves. Everything you know for sure about Jesus, somebody else told you. I know, I know, "Evangelical" has been besmirched by some evangelicals' confusion of "Evangelical" with "Right-Wing Republican." Still, one of the last things Jesus said on his way up was not, "Get real estate! Remember, location, location, location. And tell the bank you're an eleemosynary organization so you can get a better interest rate on the loan."

No. Jesus kicked us out, "Go and make disciples of all nations [*all* means all, not just the ones with whom you are most comfortable], baptizing them [because none of them is born Christian] in the name of the Father and of the Son and of the Holy Spirit [so they know that 'God' doesn't stand for some idol of their own sweet concoction], teaching them to obey everything that I've commanded you [even the hard stuff about loving and forgiving enemies]. Look, I myself will be with you every day until the end of this present age" [just to make darn sure you obey] (Matthew 28:19-20). Sent. Evangelists, all.

"Just hand people food," chided the urban minister, "We're not here to proselytize; we're here to love." I assured the anxious activist that neither he nor the homeless had anything to fear—we are mainline Protestants who would rather hand the less fortunate a bowl of soup than risk an argument over the truth. It's less disruptive to the powers-that-be to pacify the hungry by doing a little good than to testify to those in need that we're standing with them, in the cold, on the sidewalk, because Jesus stationed us here. More importantly, they are here—out of work, hungry, unhoused—not because of God. Durham and its attendant economic, political, and educational domination systems were created without help from Jesus.

It's true that witness, evangelical proclamation is in word and deed. In John's Gospel, Jesus serenely says, "I am the light of the world" (John 8:12). But Matthew has Jesus turn to that disappointing gaggle of disciples and send them saying, "You are the light of the world. . . . Let your light shine before people, so they can see the good things you do and praise your Father who is in heaven" (Matthew 5:14, 16). Us?

My buddy Walter Brueggemann notes the way that Jesus, in his acts of compassion, is prophetic, evangelical proclamation:

Compassion constitutes a radical form of criticism, for it announces that the hurt is to be taken seriously, that the hurt is not to be accepted as normal and natural but is an abnormal and unacceptable condition. . . . Thus the compassion of Jesus is to be understood not simply as a personal emotional reaction but as a public criticism in which he dares to act upon his concern against the entire numbness of his social context. Empires live

75

by numbness. . . . Thus compassion that might be seen simply as generous goodwill is in fact criticism of the system, forces and ideologies that produced the hurt. Jesus enters into the hurt and finally comes to embody it.[4]

Through compassionate, courageous, and merciful evangelical service to those on the margins, the church signals the shape of the world to come once God finally gets what God wants.

Why three AA meetings a week in the church basement? The cigarette butts! The food giveaway is a mess to clean up after. Why bother? A couple of our best givers walked when we pressured City Council for a pay raise for sanitation workers. Was that wise? Some folks really didn't appreciate our caravan to the Moral Mondays demonstrations in Raleigh. Why risk it? Letting our flickering lights shine.

Evangelical Thinking

Had you the patience and I the time, I could argue that evangelism is why we must think theology. There's a lot of boring, academic, irrelevant, theological throat-clearing and chewing-the-cud because of theology's timid, parochial introversion. Don't you find it remarkable that at a time when the church was fighting for its life, Paul tells Timothy that the most important thing he can do for First Church Ephesus is to think clearly?

When I left for Macedonia, I asked you to stay behind in Ephesus so that you could instruct certain individuals not to spread wrong teaching. They shouldn't pay attention to myths and endless genealogies. Their teaching only causes useless guessing games. . . . The goal of instruction is love from a pure heart, a good conscience, and a sincere faith. . . . some people have been distracted by talk that doesn't mean anything. They want to be teachers of Law without understanding either what they are saying or what they are talking about with such confidence. . . . They are the ungodly and the sinners. . . . They kill their fathers and mothers, and murder others (1 Timothy 1:3-9).

Allow people to believe anything that makes them happy, adrift in pointless, anthropological, nonbiblical, nonchristological, majoring-in-the-minors *guessing games*, next thing, says Paul, *they kill their fathers and mothers.*

I've been to Ephesus, one of the best sites for seeing the wonders of classical antiquity. The Temple of Hadrian and the Library of Celsus, worth a trip to Turkey. Frankly, Paul is unimpressed: in his letters, the great architectural, sculptural glories of the Ephesians are nowhere noted. Seen one pompous, pagan, government-funded shrine, you've seen 'em all, Paul seems to say to the little group huddled around the kitchen table at Timothy's grandmother's house, seditiously plotting the next steps for turning Caesar's world upside down, otherwise known as evangelism.

To a church hanging on by its fingernails, Paul says, all the more reason to be clear about the truth that sends us forth, making careful distinction between what seems right to nine-out-of-ten average Ephesians and the singular truth about God in Jesus Christ. When the church is overburdened by *people* who *have been distracted by talk that doesn't mean anything,* playing *useless guessing games instead of faithfulness to God's way of doing things* (the picture of The UMC grows clearer) pastors must be rabbis.

"We are upset that The UMC ordained a lesbian out West somewhere," was the teensy congregation's justification for leaving the denomination. This from a church that hasn't made a new Christian in three years. They'll be dead before I will, killed by *distracted talk* diverting their attention from *faithfulness to God's way of doing things.*

Paul has little sympathy with the theologically curious who waste time with *myths and endless genealogies . . . useless guessing games . . .* and *talk that doesn't mean anything.* (Why am I thinking of most PhD programs in "Religion"?) Paul's plea for theology is just what one would expect from a practical, missionary theologian who keeps close to everyday, nitty-gritty realities and therefore has little patience with spiritual flights of fancy. Theology helps the church keep the main thing, the main thing, making church as demanding, difficult, and adventuresome (that is, *missional*) as Christ intends church to be.

Every Scripture is inspired by God and is useful for teaching, for showing mistakes, for correcting, and for training character, so that the person who belongs to God can be equipped to do everything that is good (2 Timothy 3:16-17).

The kids whined about the volume of reading in my Introduction to Ordained Leadership. (Though most of the required books were written by the instructor!)

I thought about lightening up. Then, on my way to campus, listening to NPR I heard a report about the outbreak of Hansen's disease, leprosy, on the Texas/Mexico border. A beleaguered public health nurse spoke of the challenge posed by these resurgent skin diseases.

"My patients' main question is, 'Why would God do this to me? I've tried to live a good life and go to church.'"

I blew into class hysterically, "Bad theology, delivered by pastors who are too arrogant to learn the faith, is deadly! Stupid theology puts people in pain. You're going to read every page that's assigned, even the footnotes. One day, your people will thank me!"

Beware of false teaching.

Heresy hurts. Christianity is more than a set of helpful, healthy practices. It's first of all a word about God, who God is, what God's up to in the world, an external word that usually doesn't make sense when we first hear it, a word that has never easily found a home in the world. If being a Christian is the same as being a sensitive, thoughtful American with residual spiritual yearnings, who needs theology?

"I just met the God I didn't know wanted me," the sophomore said after my lecture on the Trinity. Thank you, intervening, enlivening, schooling Holy Spirit, for making my remarks mean more than I meant. Second Timothy 3:16-17 in action, this time at Duke.

Had not Jesus promised that though Golgotha cut short his lectures, he'd send his Holy Spirit to teach all the rest (John 14:26)?

Still, the way I see it, the worst theological mistakes occur in evangelism. In reaching over to speak to the world, sometimes we fall in face down. We rework the gospel into a sort of primitive technique for self-improvement, giving the world something that it already has without all the Jewish baggage. Reduce the faith to a sappy, snappy slogan that fits on a bumper sticker. Advertising masquerading as evangelism.

Theology keeps asking, "Are we talking about the God who has spoken Jesus Christ to us?" which Karl Barth said was the test question at the heart of dogmatics. The more successful a congregation in mission, the greater the need to teach, handing over the faith to new converts, helping evangelists to talk and think Christian, making theologians of us all.

There will come a time when people will not tolerate sound teaching. They will collect teachers who say what they want to hear because they are self-centered. They will turn their back on the truth and turn to myths (2 Timothy 4:3-4).

You ask, "Isn't it arrogant to try to 'convert' people, acting as if our point of view is better than theirs?"

Once asked that myself.

Then it occurred to me that the question arises from the erroneous assumption that there are innocent, untouched, ideological virgins out there whom these pushy Christians try to arm wrestle into faith. No. In the words of theologian Bob Dylan, everybody serves somebody. They've already been "converted" by some "evangelist" into an assumption about who's in charge, what's what, and where we're headed. Why abandon people to the myths of twenty-first-century capitalism and governmentally subsidized egoistic narcissism? Why fly the flag higher than the cross? Let's put our stuff on the table, compare it to theirs, and enjoy God messing with attenuated modern imaginations.

My university chaplain's eyes were opened by Robert Jenson calling classical philosophy, "ancient Greek religion." Jenson gave me the wherewithal to respond to campus philosophical cultured despisers' "I don't believe in a god," with, "I don't believe you," beginning (but sometimes ending) many conversations. For Christians of Timothy's time, baptism was intellectual rebellion against the official political and spiritual regime of paganism, Rome, Aristotle, Plato and all that.

One more thing: Recognition that our church lives in a vast, pagan-dominated mission field where our people are bombarded by bogus counter narratives of what's what, and who's who reminds us that sometimes those inside the church are in greatest need of continuing conversion, requiring a pastor with the guts to *instruct certain individuals not to spread wrong teaching.* Let the arguments begin.

It Is about the Money

Paul's commitment to applied theology explains how easily Paul moves from theological discourse to urging Timothy to teach economics. In First Timothy, Paul says less about salvation than money. (What you feel in your heart about Jesus is less theologically significant than what Jesus does with your cash?) I'm upset by what Paul says about women or enslavement when, considering the size of my 401(k), shouldn't I be as bothered by what he says to people of means like me?

They think that godliness is a way to make money! [Here's looking at you, Prosperity Gospelers.] *Actually, godliness is a great source of profit when it is combined with being happy with what you already have.* [My mother's favorite Bible verse.] *We didn't bring anything into the world and so we can't take anything out of it: we'll be happy with food and clothing.* [A really short happiness list, by our standards.] *But people who are trying to get rich fall into temptation. They are trapped by many stupid and harmful passions that plunge people into ruin and destruction.* [Talkin' 'bout you, Mar-a-Lago.] *The love of money is the root of all kinds of evil.* [Paul's just handed you your Fall Stewardship Sunday sermon for free.] *Some have wandered away from the faith and have impaled themselves with a lot of pain because they made money their goal.* [Never had a preacher call it quits because of Jesus. You'd think they would, considering our Lord's demands. Money, a chief cause of clergy exits.] (1 Timothy 6:5-10).

Scarcely stopping to draw breath, Paul rants:

Tell people who are rich at this time not to become egotistical and not to place their hope on their finances. . . . Instead, they need to hope in God, who richly provides everything for our enjoyment. Tell them to do good, to be rich in the good things they do, to be generous, and to share with others. When they do these things, they will save a treasure for themselves that is a good foundation for the future. That way they can take hold of what is truly life (1 Timothy 6:17-19).

Who says there's no judgment in the gracious gospel?

Never had a family in my congregation endangered because of somebody's same-sex marriage. No undocumented immigrant has ever harmed a teenager in my churches. As pastor to troubled blue collar families, I learned that it doesn't take much money to mess up a child.

Ripping the rich in his congregation, Basil of Caesarea puts a point on First Timothy 6: Because of Jesus, "The bread that you store up belongs to the hungry; the cloak that lies in your chest belongs to the naked; the gold that you have hidden in the ground belongs to the poor."[5]

While I want you to be theologically orthodox, one of your most important decisions in the early days of ministry is to decide how much money you need to be happy. Go ahead. Write it down, because the love of money is the root of all kinds of evil.

I doubt that Paul or Timothy had as many rich in their congregations as I've had in mine, which helps explain why I've preached less on the root of all kinds of evil than Paul. I think it's amazing that Timothy's evangelism attracted even a few of the rich. For all their materialism and stupidity, they must have been more courageous and open-minded than the moneyed whom my anemic preaching has assembled.

Come on, admit it, isn't it invigorating to watch Paul rant against the rich, thereby making clear that while he's working with them, and

81

in his letter he's working on them, never does he work for them and, because of Jesus, has a sacred responsibility to sock it to them.

As a theological student, I thought that the early church was made up mostly of the economically marginalized, a logical assumption considering how often Jesus blessed the poor and excoriated the rich. First Timothy suggests otherwise. Somehow Timothy has managed to evangelize even the rich (whom Jesus said were as difficult to pull into the kingdom of heaven as squeezing a fully loaded dromedary through the eye of a needle, Matthew 19:23-24), and train them to expect judgment and critique by their evangelizers.

The privileged well-heeled are warned not to fall prey to the many stupid and harmful passions that plunge many inhabitants of gated communities into ruin and destruction and in the same sermon urged to do good, to be rich in the good things they do, to be generous, and to share with others, giving them something good to do with the gifts they have received. While pride is the chief of the Seven Deadlies, I take a bit of it in my ability to put the squeeze on a few people of means thereby demonstrating that while the salvation of a rich dromedary is daunting, Jesus said it's possible (Matthew 19:26). Though it may be tough on the camel.

Paul urges loaded laity to do good with wealth; the world is watching. The church is a showcase of God's mission in which being redeemed sinners serve as signs of what God's love can accomplish. Israel and the church are evangelical object illustrations of God's glory. Salvation is particularly, visibly, institutionally staged in the church for the benefit of the whole world. God purposes the salvation of all, but that will not be accomplished in a way that ignores or bypasses the historical, real world economic experiment named church.

Extroverted

When I entered ministry, conservative Methodists called themselves "evangelical." At some point (blame it on Asbury Seminary) they couldn't take the heat and changed their self-designation to "tradition-alist." There's a world of difference between thinking of yourself as an extroverted, goodnewsing evangelical rather than an introverted, scru-pulous, guardian of the truth preservationist.

It's like a law of God: An introverted, self-concerned church is a congregation on the way out. Churches either grow (take in new life) or die (reassuring ourselves on the way to the cemetery, "We're not growing, but we are holding to our tradition"). As Jesus argued, the kingdom of God is known by its expansion and advance, the fruit produced by those who recklessly sling seed (Matthew 13:1-23). Paul would be baffled by our bogus attempts to defend evangelistic inept-itude: "Our church started a community garden! And hope to rent some of our unused space to a coffee shop!"

Believe me, I've looked. There's no biblical justification for an aging, dwindling congregation. Why? Goodnewsing is the *Missio Dei* and the chief confirmation of the orthodoxy of the good news is when it takes root in inhospitable soil (Matthew 13).

Pray that God will keep alive in you the evangelistic shock ["Has God's salvation gone even to the Gentiles?" (Acts 11:18)] and preserve you from the sin of attempting to give theological rationalization for death by introversion.

If you've tried handing over the gospel, people fishing (Matthew 4:19), you've already found that many are attracted to Christ but are repulsed by the sorry performance of Christ's body, the church. (And I'm not just talking about Catholic bishops or the leaders of the South-ern Baptist Convention who failed to hold clergy accountable for sexual misdeeds.) Christ pressures the church to be an institutional rendition of something the world isn't. Whenever church is limited to a single nationality, generation, race, or language, we've flunked the Acts 2, Pentecostal criterion for church. When the church sounds the same as the world, why listen? A church that chooses up sides and splits, right/left, progressive/traditionalist, Republican/Democrat (poor UMC) says to polarized America, "We're no better than you." Pick a congregation that shares your values before you came to church and call that "church," saying to the world, "Jesus Christ is Lord, but not lord enough to convene a people who look different from the world."

At first glance, First and Second Timothy seem introverted, obsessed with internal, congregational trivialities, insider baseball. A closer read reveals that Paul preaches ethics for evangelical reasons: The primary way the world sees Christ is by looking at Christ's Bride, the poor old, compromised tart. Bride of Christ, full-of-holes body of Christ, *Ecclesia* is how God saves. That's why the greatest evangelistic, missionary need is not better apologetics but the church you will lead, a visibly more faithful church that doesn't contradict Christ's appeal to ᵗʰ ᵂᵒᵣˡᵈ

Therefore, I want . . . Brace yourself. *Therefore* signals that here comes ethical exhortation arising from theological affirmation. Having nobly confessed, *There is one God and one mediator between God and humanity, the human Christ Jesus, who gave himself as a payment to set all people free* (1 Timothy 2:5-6), Paul dives into nitty-gritty, real-life ethics for an extroverted church:

Therefore, I want men to pray everywhere by lifting up hands that are holy, without anger or argument. In the same way, I want women to enhance their appearance with clothing that is modest and sensible, not with elaborate hairstyles, gold, pearls, or expensive clothes. They should make themselves attractive by doing good, which is appropriate for women who claim to honor God (1 Timothy 2:8-10).

Avoidance of angry argument among men, women's abstinence from gold, pearls, and designer clothes? Who cares, right?

Not for the missionary outpost that's a showcase of what God can do among ordinary Christians attempting *to honor God.*

So much of pastoral work seems trivial and inconsequential in the world's eyes—enduring the Finance Committee meeting, waiting for the plumber to show up and unclog the downstairs boy's toilet, an afternoon spent listening to the troubles of a fourteen-year-old, nego- tiating with the organist over next Sunday's closing hymn, sitting in your study plotting how to preach Jonah 2 without everybody getting their hackles up.

May you be given the grace to see your unglamorous pastoral work as evangelistic, missional, even prophetic as you partner with God in sending a church that's a showcase, witness, and testimony to what the Lord can do among a bunch of sinners who've been grabbed by God.

Paul says, *I was appointed a messenger, apostle, and teacher of this good news* (2 Timothy 1:11). *I'm a teacher of the Gentiles in faith and truth* (1 Timothy 2:7), implying that the test of Paul's ministry is not how well he has mollified the faithful but how well he's enlightened the pagans, in church and out.

Mission and evangelism begin in the heart of God, with Christ's determination not to withhold the truth from anyone. As Barth tried to teach me but Newbigin finally convinced me, the church has been elected by God as God's chief bearer of Christ's good news into the world, though not the exclusive beneficiary. God *wants all people to be saved and to come to a knowledge of the truth* (1 Timothy 2:4). We're servants of God's mission, never master or originator, stewards of the good news, not possessors of a privilege from which others are excluded.

What a way to get what you want out of the world. Still, it's Christ's way. All the baptized are evangelists. Apostolic. Sent to witness to the encroachment of God's reign. Our job is to equip evangelists to witness to a world that has yet to get the news. Wherever this truth is not known, Christ barges in, speaking through those whom he has sent, urgent and universal in reach, filling every empty place, fishing for all, leaping every boundary, relevant to all, binding upon all. Whether rejected or embraced, Christ's determination to get back what belongs to God is indomitable. He neither gives a rip for borders nor has he ever taken the world's rejection seriously. Thank God.

Questions from Jason Byassee, Senior Minister, Timothy Eaton Memorial Church, Toronto, and

author of twenty books on theology, biblical interpretation, church, and ministry. Jason has been an
editor for *The Christian Century* and served on the
faculty of Vancouver School of Theology.

1. Aren't you missing the force of the critique of
   evangelism? It's clever to aim it against "the rich"
   with Timothy, but it became synonymous with
   Western colonialism and destroyed cultures. Isn't
   there *something* to this critique? How would you
   respond to it?

2. Ok, I agree, reluctantly: we should evangelize.
   Now, how do we do it? Is there a place for "apologetics"—the discipline of countering outsiders'
   questions and promoting the truth of the gospel?

3. Have you seen a church (note: not an individual,
   not a country) evangelize successfully, perhaps
   despite itself? How'd it do this?

CARING WITH JESUS

The point of ministry is care for the congregation's hurts and sadness. Time spent counseling the troubled and visiting the sick validates you as a good pastor.

The pastor is the Wounded Healer of aggrieved souls.

Because we're required to work on Sundays and visit the sick and needy, pastoral work demands are excessive.

As pastor, if you don't care for yourself, nobody will.

We'll never know how Timothy's mother and grandmother reacted to his becoming a preacher/pastor/missionary. What did those near and dear say to you when you threw caution to the wind and cast your lot with Jesus?

My own dear mother, when I finally summoned the courage to admit that I might, just maybe, could possibly, perhaps be headed to seminary responded, "For what purpose, pray tell?"

"To become somebody's pastor," I answered.

"In what church?" she pressed.

"Methodist, of course."

"I was hoping you would say Presbyterian. Their pastors are erudite, fluent in Greek and Hebrew. Few Methodist preachers impress with their learnedness. I doubt this will end well." Then, to make it stick, "Pastors must cajole and flatter parishioners, patronize their congregations' every whim and, well, let's just say, it's difficult to imagine your succeeding."

When I've recounted my mother's less-than-enthusiastic comeback to my declaration of vocation, church members have said, "Wish I could have met your mother."

Christian Care

To compensate for Mother's frank assessment of my pastoral defi-
ciencies, upon graduation from seminary I took a painful yet formative quarter of Clinical Pastoral Education. Never did my CPE supervisor mention Jesus while he harped redundantly on the need to "be good listeners," "share your humanity," "go with your gut," and urged us chaplains-in-training to "lead with your feelings."

My CPE schooling took place in a euphemistically labeled "convalescent center" where nobody got better unless you count as progress a trip to the mortuary. I'm not sure that a medical center is the best place to train pastors, although CPE did give me an introduction to the institutionalized sin otherwise known as modern, high-tech medical care. I was also prepared for life in a denomination full of anxious, ailing, aging Boomers for whom death is an injustice that happens to other people. In my CPE training, because everyone under my care was terminal, they (without even trying) taught me that we need more, in our departing, than the presence of an empathetic fellow mortal, even one with a new MDiv.

First year as a pastor, when I expressed surprise at the depression, addiction, and psychological imbalance roaming in my congregation, the lay leader responded, "In this town, the well-adjusted got better things to do than church. We're stuck with what's left. What our Lord sees in 'em, maybe one day I'll know."

I consumed books on pastoral care and counseling to shield myself from being consumed by my people's omnivorous demands. Most of these books presupposed, though they lacked the guts to say it, "Since we all know that God is gone, or at least insufficiently concerned about human need, here's how pastors should care since God doesn't."

When advised by my first district superintendent, "Just love your people and everything will work out," a shudder went down my spine, knowing the limits of my love and the extent of Methodists' frequent unloveableness. Why go to seminary if ministry is just lovin' up on people who pay my salary?

Parishioners who presented me with their chronic, serious personal problems never got better because of anything I said or did, causing me to question my care because, in those salad days of ministry, I thought that changing people for the better was a realistic ministerial goal, for one so competent as I.

"Preachers smarter than you have tried to help," said one sometimes recovering, often not, alcoholic. "About all you preachers do is give a body more excuses to take a drink."

I began to be troubled that some used my pastoral care to bolster their self-delusions (otherwise known by die-hard traditionalists as "sin"). Never did I care for anyone who had the lung cancer that's caused by smoking or the high blood pressure that's due to poor lifestyle choices.

To some of my parishioners' "Why, God, did this happen to me," I had an answer, but was too compassionate (cowardly?) to give it. "Why? Because you chose to live grossly overweight," or "You drank too much," or "This is what you get when you're unfaithful to your marriage vows."

Fortunately, *Whatever Became of Sin?* arrived my second year of ministry (the same month the delusional *I'm OK—You're OK* hit the *New York Times* bestseller list).[1] Menninger's psychotherapeutic insistence on the pervasiveness of human sin helped me see what Flannery O'Connor or Wesley tried to tell me: We are rarely more self-deceptive

89

than when in pain. I became interested in the ministrations of 12 Step programs, particularly AA's notorious 4th Step. AA says it's essential that recovering alcoholics take an inventory of their character flaws and personal weaknesses (a.k.a., confession) or they won't get better.

"How come I had to go to the church basement every Wednesday night with AA to learn I'm a sinner?" a recovering alcoholic asked. Why? Because your pastor is a sentimental Methodist who needs to believe, all evidence to the contrary, that you are a nice person who's making progress, thereby bolstering my pastoral delusion that I'm a nice person who helps fellow nice people become even nicer.

When Methodists commit theological sin, sappy, sin-free senti- mentalism is *nostra culpa.*

- Sentimentality denies human enslavement to evil and sin and reduces the gospel to fantasies of earnest human striving or un- justified positive feelings about human capacity for goodness.

- Sentimentality is the illusion that once we've said something, sighed deeply, and shed an empathetic tear we've done some- thing.

- Sentimentality is the pretense of love without justice, for- giveness without reparations, incarnation without cruciform atonement, mission without risk, salvation without vocation, the gracious word of the Lord free of judgment or reproof by the Lord. We are fine just as we are, thank you, pedaling as fast as we can, without need of costly divine renovation.

Rather than talk about a God who dares to justify the ungodly (Romans 4:5), we, the willfully innocent, lapse into degraded Pela- gianism: We are basically good people who, tomorrow, could be even better.

Kierkegaard castigated the Danish church for mawkishly imbibing "the cordial drivel of family life," as if Jesus's mission is to boost our marriages and families. Sentimental glorification of the family, said the Melancholy Dane, is self-love transposed, "mediocrity"—"nauseating . . . homey, civil togetherness"—substituted for salvation.

Sentimentality: gospel substitute of the moment. A mass killing? Hand out candles, have a vigil, link arms in the darkness, declare "this community comes together in times like these," and call that care.

Racism? "Find somebody of another race and just have a conversation. Discover the richness of this person's diverse experience. You'll be blessed."

The essence of Christianity? "It all boils down to, 'Love your neighbor as yourself.'"

Death? "She will live on in our memories."

Tragedy? "Everything happens for a reason."

Mainline church dissolution? "Gracious exit and charitable departure," says the bishop who refuses to risk honest conversation with unhappy people.

I once heard a church official examine candidates for ordination with, "Do you have a pastor's heart?" I made a Christologically based counter proposal: "Have you a theologian's brain and a rabble-rouser's smart mouth that equips you for this entanglement? Above all, are you squeamish about telling people the truth, tackling your sin and theirs, no matter the pain?"

I'm huffy over the sins of an adulterous, thieving, lying former U.S. president, as if he were an aberration. Then comes along Paul telling the Romans that "All have sinned and fall short of God's glory" (Romans 3:23). I've met the enemy: me. A near majority of white Americans (and not just in Iowa) think the rascal ought again be president. Brush up your hamartiology.

Sentimentality cannot account for the gaggle of ungodly people Jesus gathers to himself, otherwise known as church. Jesus is why preachers care for congregations by being in a potentially contentious relationship with them. If Jesus wanted only to heal and love them (as they define healing and love), ministry could be relegated to a "helping profession." Church is better than a hospital. It's the body of Christ in motion, a bunch of sinners convened by God to hear and then to propagate a royal proclamation.

If your leadership of evangelism is effective, your church will be full of the same incomprehension, cowardice, disbelief, self-pity, and rebellion that arise when any human gathering is assaulted by the Word.

And so will you. When the Eucharist is celebrated clergy receive Communion first, the pastor being chief among sinners. We preachers meet no resistance to the Word among our congregants that does not lie within our own hearts. My uneasiness with some of the things Paul says to Timothy about the rich, or about lousy theologians, show that though I believe Scripture can be God's word, when it's God's word to me, or God's judgment that I must hand over to some parishioner in pain, I wish it weren't God's word.

Leadership gurus tell pastors we must win the trust of our congregations before we can truly lead. Paul tells the Ephesians that they ought to trust us to speak "the truth with love" (Ephesians 4:15). How can I be sure that my professed "love" is not just a cover for my self-love and co-dependence upon the whims of those from whom I crave affirmation? Sometimes my "I love my people" means "I love me and want to use them to love myself even more."

Still, by the grace of God, we pastors manage occasionally to pain the people we love and thereby risk being put in pain by people who love us. Church, worthy of the name.

"Everybody loved you as our pastor," declared a leader of one of my former congregations when I bumped into her at a Billy Joel concert. "Except of course, Joan Smith."

"Joan? She adored me. Served as the youth coordinator," I said defensively. "Invited me to her barbecues."

"That's news?" she marveled. "She loathed you. You're the preacher who told her the truth about her son."

In our sentimental paternalistic/maternalistic attempts to protect Jesus from his crucifiers, we tuck Jesus into people's individual consciences, make him personal, helpful, and empathetic, robbing Christ of his political intent. Pandering to their self-pity, we preach as if their bottomless need is the equivalent of a word from God.

Since Schleiermacher, many have attempted to rescue the gospel from the onslaughts of modernity by reducing the cosmic Christian faith into the subjective, experiential, and individual. Jesus's uniquely communal, sacramental approach to salvation (church) is thereby made incomprehensible. Stay-at-home, "virtual worship" passed off as the real thing. Pastoral care relegated to one-on-one counseling; leadership to personal relationships.

By the nature of our work, pastors are constantly exposed to folks at their most miserable, some of them desperate. Sick people get a free pass; they can be as impolite and difficult as they please, demanding that the whole world revolve around their pain. In a society whose hospitals are bigger than our cathedrals, sickness is the most interesting thing that happens to many. Doctors are too busy to listen, therapists are expensive. Nobody but their pastor to handle their complaint.

Rather than be a beachhead of subversive resident aliens preparing for the coup (a.k.a., the kingdom of heaven), church is reduced to a therapeutic sanctuary where we receive our spiritual pep talk for the week. "What works for me" trumps both "progressive" and "traditional." Consumers of care drift, searching for a congregation that "meets my needs," "matches my lifestyle," "works for me," or "aligns with my values."

When an alleged "Bible Study" group begins with a twenty-minute sick report, I doubt that the Bible will be allowed to say anything except what can be murmured to someone stuck in a nursing home.

No pastor is thanked for confronting adulterers and attempting to rouse them to repentance; all pastors are praised for hanging out at the hospital, though none of us have had medical training.

At the end of a six-hour stint at Greenville General, as I made my dog-tired way down the steps to the exit, I was thrilled to bump into a doctor whom I knew, confident that I looked so bushed that even he would get my message: "Look at me! Though I make half your salary (I was in school almost as long as you). I'm the world's best, hard-working, obstinately caring pastor ever."

Unimpressed by my do-gooder fatigue the doc asked, "Have you always had a need to be needed, or did that come with seminary?"

My novice conviction that ministry is mostly about empathetic caring, without Christological conditioning and discipline, wilted.

I remembered James Dittes, professor of pastoral care, asking, at sherry hour in the YDS common room, "So many of our students come to seminary saying they plan to do pastoral counseling and chaplaincy. I hope it's not because they think these are central activities of Christian ministry. I suppose it's because counseling, work with the wounded, and care of the psychologically damaged, are the last socially approved activities of pastors."

This from a guy who teaches pastoral counseling.

At the time, I thought Dittes was being too tough on us aspirant caregivers. Ministry changed my mind.

Caring with Jesus

It's not for nothing that letters like 1 and 2 Timothy are called "pastoral epistles." An experienced congregational caregiver advises a colleague in a more expansive notion of care than today's "pastoral care." Tell me, do you hear an ounce of therapeutic unctuousness in Paul's boosting of Timothy?

I'm reminding you to revive God's gift that is in you through the laying on of my hands. God didn't give us a spirit that is timid but one that is powerful, loving, and self-controlled. . . . Make an effort to present yourself to God as a tried-and-true worker, who doesn't need to be ashamed but is one who interprets the message of truth correctly (2 Timothy 1:6-7; 2:15).

"Just share yourself," somebody had advised. "The Ministry of Presence." "Don't preach, listen." "Your role is not to fix them or give solutions; you are midwife, helping them discover their answers for themselves." Welcomed advice since none of it required any growth on my part. It also relieved me from taking responsibility for my people and their problems. Then ministry changed my mind.

I began to find a nice way of asking those who came to me for counsel, "Why come to me with your pain over your [failing marriage, addicted spouse, erectile dysfunction (I kid you not), peanut allergy (yes, even that), or (of course) resentment of your father]? I'm a pastor, not a therapist."

Often we would mutually discover that they sought me out, not because I was free and obligated to hang with them. They had an inchoate sense that somehow theirs was a God problem, a hunch that God was mixed up in their mess, had some explaining to do, or was waiting for them in that frightening gap between sickness and health. Though their culture offered few means for construing their lives other than psychological, they had the good sense to know that, at bottom, their pain had theological significance. What a joy to be invited to do practical theology with them.

When Duke invited me (way too soon) to teach courses in liturgy and worship, being a Methodist I knew that few Free Church seminarians gave a rip about either. The sole ministerial activity that excited them was pastoral care. So my first summer at Duke I wrote *Worship as Pastoral Care* hoping to lure them back into the chancel.

"What difference does it make that we don't just care for people in their need but care *in the name of Jesus*?" What does the church actually claim it's doing when we administer liturgies of birth, death, dying, and marriage? I commended leadership of the sacraments as a means of rescuing caring from the clutches of consumeristic, self-help, godless, culturally sanctioned, governmentally subsidized, psychological notions of care. Besides, the gospel is not first of all a means of helping, as we'd like to be helped, or meeting our needs, as we define them. The gospel is a claim about reality, a.k.a., God.

Modern, reasonably affluent North Americans have psychological problems because them's the only problems the government pays for. We've lost a language for more interesting assessments than, "I'm depressed." Church is, "Come, sit close to me so I can tell you all about my wounds." We present Jesus as among us to help us be happy. Though CPE, pastoral care, group grope, spill-your-guts types despised it, *Worship as Pastoral Care* was the Academy of Parish Clergy's book-of-the-year.

In the actual day-to-day practice of ministry, I learned (let's say it one more time) there's no good reason to be in ministry other than God, and there's no way to survive and thrive that's not dependent upon a crucified God who loves to raise the dead. We care in Christ's name for what he cares about, in the way he cares, or our pastoral care is, well, careless.

Called to Care

Am I cutting too close to the bone? Stanley Hauerwas and I published a conversation on pastoral care in Jesus's name.[2] Although working clergy found our article spot on, a few academics took offense: A professor at Asbury Seminary called us "unkind" in our "withering critique." A retired Princeton prof dismissed us as "grumpy," "uncaring" for the woes of worn-out clergy and complained that our article was a word "out of season."

Throughout my ministry, when I've dared to speak against racism, my critics always have said, "Don't disagree with what you said, just wish you hadn't said it now." Which explains Paul urging Timothy to speak truth in season and out (2 Timothy 4:1-5).

A Yale sub-dean, calling me "insensitive" and "unloving," urged students to avoid my Beecher Lectures. A Duke sociologist put us down as "un-pastoral" (a word?), "deeply flawed" without saying why. No critic mentioned Jesus or showed interest in having a theological discussion about the difference it makes that the recipients of our care are the baptized who, even in their pain, are called by and accountable to God. Nor did our academic denigrators show awareness of the privileged, North American, cultural, economic, racial biases infecting their versions of Jesus-free "pastoral care."

A pastor who used our article to good effect among the staff of his urban congregation noted, "None of your critics are pastors. Which may be why they failed to notice your linkage of care and vocation."

Jesus has bigger fish to fry than my happiness. Or yours. You got problems? Come to Jesus; he'll give you problems you would not have had if he had not enlisted you. Trust me, over the course of my ministry, Jesus has gotten me into more trouble than I could have caused on my own.

Bonhoeffer noted that when he went to a psychiatrist, "The psychiatrist views me as if there were no God." To the psychiatrist "I can only be a sick man." A pastor views me as a fellow disciple standing "before the judging and merciful God in the Cross of Jesus Christ."[3]

What's good news is that in Christ—the One who matched his reckless call of those four fishermen by risking a summons to you and me—God is reconciling the world to God (2 Corinthians 5:19). He promised the fishermen, not happiness, health, or hope but rather that he would teach them to "catch people," concerning themselves with someone else's salvation. Calling, vocation is the way Christ saves, not only forgiving our sins but also giving us a job more demanding than self-care.

Here I want publicly to acknowledge my indebtedness to the Black church and friends who, usually without even trying, corrected my white, bourgeoisie attenuated notions of church and ministry. The Black church, at its best, has never been under the illusion that America was a benign environment for making and keeping their children Christian. Centuries of white supremacist rule (by white Christians) has delivered them of any sentimental notion that Black folk can survive or be free without the blood of Jesus.

Some of us white folks feel guilty because we are. God created you to feel stress if you have a hundred-thousand-dollar mortgage. Our anxiety, tension, and despair call not for empathy but gospel-induced liberation from the delusion of the American dream. Pity the poor pastor who attempts to heal wounds "lightly" with superficial bromides (Jeremiah 6:14).

I know a church that declared a "Year of Lament," after the death of George Floyd, focusing on various lament psalms, just to show how sad white people were. I told them they should have declared a season of confession, truth-telling, and repentance assisted by the imprecatory and penitential psalms. Pastoral care worthy of the name.

Without Christological discipline, we are in danger of producing church folk who can't tell the difference between Rotarian and Christian, nice people who treat their pastor like a therapist on the ~~hurt, who act as if all their wounds are of interest to Christ. Secu~~lar (that is, godless) definitions of human attenuate our imaginations. Christ's perennial vocation, "Change your hearts and lives!" followed by, "Come, follow me," then "Go into all the world," "Catch people" becomes incomprehensible.

Jesus Christ thinks nothing of calling hurting, sorrowing, frail, and sinful people anyway. Sickness—mental or physical—misfortune or dearth of talent don't deter Jesus from assembling people as his body. Even more outrageous, he assigns us roles in his mission that are beyond our abilities. I probably wouldn't have done it this way, if saving me and the world were left up to me; but, like it or not, it's uniquely Christ's way.

That's why the wounds that Paul cares about are those inflicted by his vocation as one appointed a messenger, apostle, and teacher of this good news. This is also why I'm suffering the way I do, but I'm not ashamed (2 Timothy 1:11).

I'm too caring ever to say, when you are the victim of vocationally induced suffering, *Accept your share of suffering like a good soldier of Christ Jesus* (2 Timothy 2:3). However, Paul says it: *In fact, anyone who wants to live a holy life in Christ Jesus will be harassed* (2 Timothy 3:12). I'm sure that the heckling I've endured from toadies of the Global Methodist Church would hardly count as harassment in the eyes of Paul. Still, it suggests that even I could be a messenger, apostle, and teacher of this good news.

Lest I sound negative about our vocation, let me testify that my vocation has made me a better human. I've still got a long way to go and too little time to get there, but trust me, you would not have wanted to know me before God made me the sort of person who thinks nothing of arising in the middle of the night, summoned by the bleating of one of my flock, getting dressed, and going out and being a pastor even when it doesn't personally please me to do so. While I'm not as good a caregiver as Kate Bowler makes me out to be, I'm not as bad as Beverly Gaventa says.[4] Time and again, caring conversation with one of my sheep has rescued me from wallowing in self-concern or fretting over my finitude. Look at me. Lots of old guys have nothing to do on a Friday night but the bottle or PBS. Here I sit, gleefully dispensing advice to a younger pastor, whether you wanted it or not. You and the Lord know how to make an old guy happy.

God Matters

Temptations abound for pastors to do pastoral care as if God doesn't matter. The world is determined to make being American (or white, cisgender, wounded, Millennial, Progressive, and so on) more determinative than baptism. Otherwise innocuous terms like "self-care," "balance," "Sabbath-keeping," "boundaries," "empathy," "trauma," and "wounds" must be interrogated, redefined, maybe even discarded, by the mission of Jesus. Therefore, the greatest challenge in pastoral care is not to align our care with the most recent insights of psychology or human development, but rather to come alongside the God who cares for God's people so that they are equipped to participate in God's mission to God's world.

A successful man of means comes to Jesus and asks what he's got to do to earn eternal life. Mark says that Jesus "loved him."

"You are lacking one thing. Go, sell what you own, and give the money to the poor. Then you will have treasure in heaven. And come, follow me." Just about the only instance of Jesus ever having said to have loved an individual.

"But the man was dismayed at this statement and went away saddened, because he had many possessions" (Mark 10:21-22). He left depressed. (A pastoral counselor buddy calls depression "an ecclesiogenic illness.") This, the sole case of the Stranger on the Shore inviting someone to be his disciple and the person saying no. The reason for his refusal? Money.

Here's my question: What is pastoral care and counseling in the
~~ ~~~ ~~ ~~~ ~~~~ ~~ ~~~ ~~~~~

Although the rich man refused Jesus's vocation, I wonder if Jesus meant his invitation as a gift? In a culture where few have a project more important than themselves and their immediate family, where our collective fantasy is the myth of self-aggrandizement, it's liberating to hear the truth that our lives are not our own (Psalm 100:3). We don't get to be the author of our stories. It's God's self-assignment to make our lives mean what we can never make them mean, even with good therapy. Focusing upon the health needs of congregants, soothing the disquiet of the upwardly mobile (Mark 10:25 be damned) is easier (but less adventuresome and ultimately less rewarding) than the truthful teaching that Paul presses on Timothy.

Trophimus has the distinction of being the only sick person Paul names in his letters to Timothy (2 Timothy 4:20). Paul brings him up, not out of concern for Trophimus's condition but rather to explain why Paul left him behind in Miletus. You're in our thoughts and prayers Trophimus, but your maladies will not deter the mission. Bye.

Call me sentimental, but I thank God that I entered ministry in the early Seventies when, returning to the fray that Jesus was fomenting in legally segregationist South Carolina, I got to be on the front lines where the battle raged, a.k.a., Trinity UMC. In those heady first days of ministry, the racial sin that I shared with my congregation was self-evident and care for my people meant finding some way to resist my innate desire to please so that I was free to speak the truth.

Self-Care

Clergy "self-care" is all the rage. Center yourself on yourself, keep Sabbath, unplug, be good to yourself, breathe deeply, light a candle, meditate, explore your wounds, contemplate, and disconnect from those cloying, carping, boundary-disrespecting laity. Vacation your way into perseverance in ministry.

The tautology, self-care, is a thinly disguised attempt to give theological justification for bourgeois efforts to tame a living, demanding God. Privileged, powerful people enjoy thinking of ourselves as terribly overworked. When you are on top, capable, committed, caring, and concerned, with your MDiv, having to save the world all by yourself, so deeply sensitive to others' pain, it leads to fatigue, doesn't it?

Don't let me hear you talk about the need for a good "life-work balance." Balance is the atheist delusion that your life is under your control. Hands laid upon our heads make pastors' lives less important than our work, rendering us unable neatly to separate "life" from "work." Vocation throws off balance the modern, essentialist, narcissistic myth that we are most truly ourselves when we de-role, stripping ourselves of commitments and responsibility for anyone but ourselves.

Jesus was a well-documented Sabbath breaker. "Centering" (only dead animals are found in the middle of the road), "life-work balance" (nobody accused Jesus of that) fails to do justice to the peculiarity of the called-for life.

To be brutally honest, pastors who feel oppressed by the duties of ministry ought to consider if they are, 1. So unskilled in the arts of leadership that they make Jesus look bad by implying that his summons is unbearable, or, 2. Lack the gifts and the call by God to be a pastor. If my doctor began my consultation by complaining of needy patients and her job's insufferable stress, I would take my prostate exam elsewhere.

"You'll not hear me complain about how hard I'm working," said one of my students a year into pastoral ministry. "Young adult unemployment in this county is over 30 percent. I've got folks who would give anything for a stressful job." Thanks, Jesus and the bishop, for forcing clerics into situations that chasten our clericalism.

> Thanks for your email. You have attempted to contact me while I'm on Sabbath. Being your pastor is soul-draining work so Thursdays I free myself from the clutches of you demanding laity and get back in touch with God, sitting alone in silence with a latte. I hope you will be more respectful of my boundaries by not calling me on Thursdays.
> Fridays are my day off.
> If your mother has just died, call the church office and maybe someone can help.
> Please be more considerate of my Sabbath-keeping in the future.
> Blessings.
> Pastor Barb

That's more or less the email bounce back I received from a pastor who gives clergy self-care a bad name.

Timothy is the recipient of Pauline pastoral care:

Accept your share of suffering like a good soldier of Christ Jesus. Nobody who serves in the military gets tied up with civilian matters, so that they can please the one who recruited them. [Military, the best analogy for ministry?] *Also in the same way, athletes don't win unless they follow the rules.* [Jocks play by the rules. No pain, no gain.] *A hardworking farmer should get the first share of the crop.* [Surprise, ministry is a job.]. . . . *Remember Jesus Christ, who was raised from the dead and descended from David. This is my good news.* [Easy, in the press of caregiving, to suffer Christological amnesia.] *This is the reason I'm suffering to the point that I'm in prison like a common criminal.* [Jesus Christ, raised from the dead, is the cause of Paul's criminalization?] *But God's word cannot be imprisoned* [Antidote to pastoral despair? Preaching!] (2 Timothy 2:3-6, 8-9).

Accept your share of suffering. Having suffered so little in my own ministry, I have some explaining to do.

At our seminary, students are required to undergo "Spiritual Formation." What's that? "It's when we sit around and talk about how tough it is to be in seminary and about the need for rest to keep us from going nuts when we're pastors."

Jesus restrained me from preaching, "Trust me, nobody on this faculty can hurt you as deeply as the average layperson. Take heart. There's no recent report of a Methodist preacher working themselves to death. Besides, Jesus is notorious for his disregard for the Fourth Commandment."

While Paul believes in spiritual formation, it's not the kind offered at seminary:

Train (Greek: *gumnase*) *yourself for a holy life! While physical training has some value, training in holy living is useful for everything. . . . Don't let anyone look down on you because you are young. Instead, set an example for the believers through your speech, behavior, love, faith, and by being sexually pure. Until I arrive, pay attention to public reading, preaching, and teaching. Don't neglect the spiritual gift in you that was given through prophecy when the elders laid hands on you. Practice these things, and live by them so that your progress will be visible to all. Focus on working on your own development and on what you teach. If you do this, you will save yourself and those who hear you* (1 Timothy 4:7-8, 12-16).

Ask yourself: What spiritual formation is best suited for those who must tell the truth about God (a.k.a., Jesus Christ) to those who often would rather not hear? *Don't neglect the spiritual gift in you that was given through prophecy when the elders laid hands on you.*

Just doing your pastoral duties can be an effective means of self-care. Getting out of the office, dodging the soul-deadening routine of parish administration, and being out and about among God's people (church folk or not), is a window into the world *extra ecclesia*. Sermon preparation gets a shove. I see my folk amid their quotidian cares and fumbling attempts to live out their baptism. I am reminded that the proper business of Christians is not volunteering to help the pastor tidy up down at the church. It's joining Christ in mission in the world.

Due to the disastrous subordination of some Christians to the role of "laity," sometime in the fourth century, many laity eagerly dump their baptismal responsibilities—to pray for and visit the sick, to bind up wounds, to reach out to the forgotten, and to sit with the suffering—upon the clergy.

In my last congregation, uneasy about the amount of time I spent with alcoholics, as well as my inadequacies to offer effective help, I assembled three recovering alcoholics.

"Have you had training in addiction counseling?" one asked. "We know a lot more about alcohol than you. Learned the hard way. Let us take this off your plate."

The next time I encountered someone in the congregation who was either addicted or who loved someone who was, I was able to say, "I'll ask one of your fellow church members to call you. You may be surprised. You are free to refuse to talk to them about your problem. But if you do, you'll miss a wonderful opportunity to get the help you need."

Jesus Saves

Though unintended, detrimental for pastors was Henri Nouwen's book *Wounded Healer* that appeared my second year of ministry.[5] Nouwen eloquently noted how a pastor's "wounds"—personal misfortunes and difficulties—could be helpful in caring for our people. Don't present yourself as the all-sufficient, successful saint; share your human-all-too-human vulnerabilities and liabilities with your congregation.

Nouwen's well-received thesis lacked biblical or theological basis. Vocation, not woundedness, puts you in ministry. Conceiving of pastors as "wounded healers" leads to role confusion. Pastors' care of our people has unique power because it is in the name of wounded, incarcerated, bleeding *Jesus Christ, who was raised from the dead and descended from David.* Christ's wounds are more telling than ours. Jesus sent out the apostles with a message more interesting than, "I'm a hurt human too, which qualifies me to help. Where does it hurt?"

What Jesus said was, "All who want to come after me must say no to themselves, take up their cross daily, and follow me" (Luke 9:23). No false advertising. Not content with mere healing of wounds, Jesus allowed himself to be wounded by and for us so that, no matter how deeply we've suffered, our woundedness will not utterly determine our destiny.

Must we go over this again? Yes, we do. Unlike your average care provider, pastoral care binds up the saint's wounds in order to send them back into the scuffle caused by Christ's determination to save sinners, only sinners.

By the way, if you are tempted to strut your authenticity with pastoral self-display of your personhood, wounded or otherwise, please note: Paul rarely indulges in self-disclosure (far less than I have exposed myself in this book!) except to boast, *I'm the biggest sinner of all* (1 Timothy 1:15).

Sometimes clerical misbehavior is excused with, "After all, pastors are only human." Few of the laity in my congregations, having encountered the shabby reality of my personhood, need be reminded that I'm not divine. What they, and I, must remember is that pastors are persons on whom hands have been laid so that, hereafter, when anybody advises, "Just be yourself," we won't know exactly what that means. My "self" is complicated by, being messed with, and is accountable to the call of Christ.

I'm reminding you to revive God's gift that is in you through the laying on of my hands. God didn't give us a spirit that is timid but one that is powerful, loving, and self-controlled. . . . Make an effort to present yourself to God as a tried-and-true worker, who doesn't need to be ashamed but is one who interprets the message of truth correctly (2 Timothy 1:6, 7; 2:15).

Knowing that Jesus, not you, saves, guards against the depleting delusion that you are the answer to their problems. Here, I admit indebtedness to the alcoholics in my congregations who taught me the limits of my ability to make their lives turn out right.

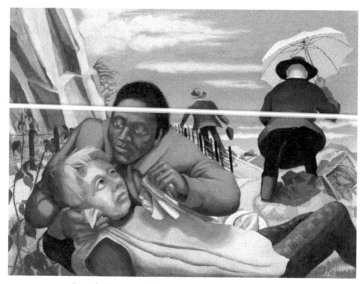

Dinah Roe Kendall, *The Good Samaritan*, 1994

On the day when he was supposed to be keeping Sabbath, Jesus healed a man and then told the carping crowd that whether he healed or not, "My Father is still working, and I am working too" (John 15:17). How often, when I've failed to be patient or sufficiently resourceful with a needy sibling of Christ, my consolation has been John 5:17. Thank God, we don't work solo.

Paul expands Timothy's work list, *Avoid foolish and thoughtless discussions, since you know that they produce conflicts. God's slave* [outrageous designation for a church leader] *shouldn't be argumentative but should be kind toward all people, able to teach, patient, and should correct opponents with gentleness.* [Then Paul adds,] *Perhaps God will change their mind and give them a knowledge of the truth. They may come to their senses and escape from the devil's trap that holds them captive to do his will* (2 Timothy 2:23-26). In other words, we work under the expectation that our people and their problems are God's joyful self-assignment. Though my help may be futile, *Perhaps God will change their mind and give them a knowledge of the truth. They may come to their senses.* Our care is a mirror of, a prelude to, preparation for the long-term care that only Christ can give.

After telling Timothy, *Make an effort to present yourself to God as a tried-and-true worker, who doesn't need to be ashamed but is one who interprets the message of truth correctly* (2 Timothy 2:15), Paul becomes tangled in a metaphor about bowls. *In a mansion, there aren't just gold and silver bowls but also some bowls that are made of wood and clay. Some are meant for special uses, some for garbage. So if anyone washes filth off themselves, they will be set apart as a "special bowl." They will be useful to the owner of the mansion for every sort of good work* (2 Timothy 2:20-21). Which means?

Ah, we bowls of garbage, cracked pots of clay (2 Corinthians 4:7), wounded healers, we are made special, set apart, useful, not because of our genius for care but because the owner of the rambunctious, rambling, always-in-need-of-repair mansion called church has set us apart *for every sort of good work.*

Questions from Joni Sancken, Butler Chair of Homiletics & Hermeneutics, Vancouver School of Theology, author of *All Our Griefs to Bear: Responding with Resilience after Collective Trauma.*

1. I've seen pastors either provide private attention, care, and counseling, feeding off the thankfulness and dependency of people in need (as you note). On the other hand, some pastors minister to those facing effects of serious trauma, mental illness, and addiction by making referrals to professionals,

sidestepping serious theological work, implying that Jesus and the body of Christ have little to offer amid crushing human experiences. How can pastors avoid both of these extremes?

2. How can clergy and congregations work with mental health professionals who may not be faith-based? Can we bear witness to Jesus's complex saving work in the webs of community and care that surround suffering members?

3. Stigma and shame can increase suffering. How can pastors protect the privacy of members and actively work to break down these barriers that prevent the church from living into its calling?

STIRRING THE POT

> Church should be a placid sanctuary. A pastor keeps the congregation peaceful and gets everyone to the table, on the same page, marching in the same direction. A conflicted, divided congregation is evidence that the pastor is not a skilled leader.
>
> If you have an ingratiating personality, it is possible to spend your life working with Jesus without being hurt by or for Jesus.

"I'm the pot stirrer," an Iowa pastor responded after I asked, "How would you characterize your ministry?"

She explained. "When you cook soup, leave it simmering on the back of the stove. For the rest of the day, when you pass through the kitchen, stir the pot."

In his letters to Timothy, Paul takes an already boiling cauldron, turns up the heat, and stirs the pot.

Interviewing pastors for my *Don't Look Back: Methodist Hope for What Comes Next,* I asked, "Why are you surreptitiously swiping your congregation from the Connection that produced and educated you?"

A frequent response was, "I'm so tired of denominational conflict. My congregation is seceding because we want a church where some things are fixed and settled without constant contention, folks are on the same page, and there's consensus."

Pugnacious Paul retorts: "If even I couldn't figure out how to create an untroubled, unified, calm congregation full of compliant, cooperative saints, you can't."

Anybody can see that Timothy's is a broken, divided, contentious church. All the more amazing that belligerent Paul shows little interest in reconciliation or healing of Ephesian divisions.

First Timothy begins with a bang: *Timothy, my child, I'm giving you these instructions based on the prophecies that were once made about you. So if you follow them, you can wage a good war. . . .* [Paul instructs Timothy in order to arm him to wage a good war.] *Some people have ruined their faith because they refused to listen to their conscience, such as Hymenaeus and Alexander.* [Ready, aim, fire!] *I've handed them over to Satan* [Translated from the apostolic: "To hell with 'em."] *so that they can be taught not to speak against God* [I bet that H and A thought they were arguing with Paul; he accuses them of speaking *against God.*] (1 Timothy 1:18-20).

Although in his second letter Paul told Timothy that he *shouldn't be argumentative but should be kind toward all people, able to teach, patient, and should correct opponents with gentleness* (2 Timothy 2:24-25), in his first epistle, the gloves are off: *Compete in the good fight of faith* (1 Timothy 6:12). A no-holds-barred smack down: *If anyone teaches anything different and doesn't agree with sound teaching about our Lord Jesus Christ and teaching that is consistent with godliness, that person is conceited* [*typhoomai,* "full of smoke"]. *They don't understand anything but have a sick obsession with debates and arguments. This creates jealousy, conflict, verbal abuse, and evil suspicions. There is constant bickering between people whose minds are ruined and who have been robbed of the truth* (1 Timothy 6:3-5). Stir that pot.

Sure, I've made snide wisecracks to church folks but, even in my most unguarded moments, never have I taken Paul's tone. Where did I get the naive notion that congregational life ought to be unperturbed? Not from the pastoral epistles.

Although as a student I enjoyed the heat of the debate, protest, and cross-generational ruckus of the Sixties, both in the classroom and on the streets, once in church, I embraced the fantasy that a good church ought to be tranquil. A conflicted congregation is a sign of ministerial screw up.

Working with Jesus, and the Scripture he engendered, changed my mind.

Troublemaker

I had to learn that there is crisis, controversy, and quarrelling in the church, among Ephesians or Greenvillians, not only because church people can be difficult (which they often are) and not because pastors are sinners too (of course we are) but because of Jesus Christ the Troublemaker he is.

Paul admits, no, boasts, that he was the biggest sinner of all. As Luke tells it (Acts 9), Church Enemy Number One, Saul, got to be Chief Missionary to the Gentiles only by being violently cast down on the Damascus Road, blinded, muted, and all round troubled by the risen Christ. No record of Paul ever having served jail time or beaten within an inch of his life until he was *appointed to be a preacher and apostle of this testimony—I'm telling the truth and I'm not lying! I'm a teacher of the Gentiles in faith and truth* (1 Timothy 2:7). Sinner though he was, it was Paul's vocation that put Paul in greatest peril.

On his way to save Judaism from wacko followers of the Way, Saul is assaulted by the risen Christ. Violently cast down, he vainly hides his eyes from the blinding light. Though dressed like a soldier, his armament is pathetic against the onslaught of Christ. Chaotic figures tumble out of the picture's frame. A bolting horse stamps menacingly close. One of Saul's companions reaches toward him, but an angel holds him back as if to say, "Let him be. Once Jesus calls, there's no helping."

111

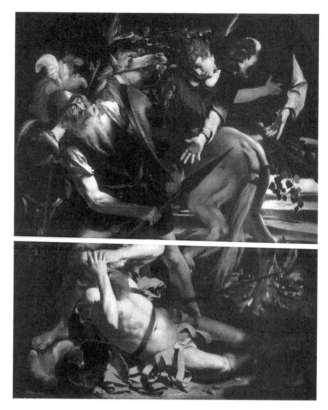

Caravaggio, *The Conversion of St. Paul,* Odescalchi Balbi Collection of Rome

Had my own vocation been as ferocious as Paul's, would I have been surprised that ministry means trouble?

I despised my R.O.T.C. stint in the Army, which may be why I'm turned off by Paul's frequent, unashamed use of martial images to characterize service in the name of the Prince of Peace. Still, maybe the military metaphors are meant to say that some church fights are worth having, fires need lighting, and pots need stirring

It's a challenge to establish irrefutable historical evidence for most details of the earthly ministry of Jesus. One thing on which historians enjoy consensus is that Jesus was crucified. Though the Romans crucified many Jews, why would Romans torture somebody to death for quietly keeping Sabbath or placidly helping folks adjust to imperial rule? Something about Jesus made government and religious authorities collude to shut him up. From the first, when King Herod heard of Jesus's birth, "he was troubled, and everyone in Jerusalem was troubled with him" (Matthew 2:3).

Luke makes a similar political point by reporting that the angelic messengers bypassed the palace and went straight to poor shepherds working the nightshift, arousing them with, "Glory to God in heaven, and on earth peace among those whom he favors" (Luke 2:14). I'm told that's a paraphrase of the greeting that preceded Caesar Augustus's royal proclamations to the inhabitants of Rome's occupied territories. The angels announce that there's a new emperor in town.

Expect trouble.

Once God publicly declared, "I'll be their God and they will be my people" (Genesis 17:7; Exodus 6:7; Ezekiel 34:24), casting God's lot with the likes of us, there was bound to be strife, considering who God is and who we are.

Preach the word. Be ready to do it whether it is convenient or inconvenient (2 Timothy 4:2). When you preach for, about, or with rabble rouser Jesus, expect some, well, as Paul puts it, "inconvenience." Some church trouble is due to people being in the pain that comes from being human. Church is personal, relational, and emotional. A high percentage of those with whom we work are beleaguered by physical or mental misfortune. Sometimes they take out their offense about the cards life dealt them by beating up on their pastor. It takes guts to admit your anger at God for life not turning out as you wanted; vent your resentment upon God's field rep.

There are deep political divisions among white Americans. *Jealousy, conflict, verbal abuse, . . . evil suspicions . . . constant bickering* (1 Timothy 6:4-5). So some Christians, unable to distinguish between their pastor and the evil suspicions provoked by the dark web, heap verbal abuse upon the one whom God called to care.

Paul doesn't worry about generic human illness, political problems, or social injustice. Church trouble, collateral damage caused by following Jesus Christ, most interests Paul.

Time and again, as I sat in my study brooding over some ministerial calamity, Jesus has found a way to say, "You're surprised? My sermon turned my hometown congregation into a murderous mob. Luke 4. You can look it up. Surely you know where my many acts of healing and compassionate pastoral care landed me. Oh, that's right, you are a graduate of an accredited ATS seminary, so you have discovered a way to preach the gospel without getting smacked."

To be honest, some discord within the congregation is not due to

say that I'm preaching, or leading, or praying for them when lots that I do is attributable to my own insecurity, pride, presumption and, well, sin. My vaunted service to them is the way I serve myself. In short, I curve the whole world in on me (Luther's definition of sin), cranking out one idol after another (Calvin's notion of sin), warping the church's mission into self-puffery.

Maybe that's why when Paul earlier narrated his autobiography in Philippians 3, he boasted of being a "Hebrew of the Hebrews," and "blameless" (Philippians 3:5-6). But after the self-awareness he's gained as a missionary church planter, he's "the biggest sinner of all" (1 Timothy 1:15).

I failed to appreciate the extent of my deceit, cowardice, vanity, and sloth until my congregation made me look in the mirror of truth, forcing me to admit that though I'm not the biggest sinner of all, I'm one of the most impressive in this church.

"You don't say everything you say out of love for Jesus," was a sullen congregant's response to my rebuke of his racism. Don't you just hate it when God transforms a moral scoundrel into your truthful preacher?

My first ministerial experience was as summer-student-intern-preacher at the Pirateland Family Campground in Myrtle Beach. I kid you not. Preaching to campers on their way to the beach on Sunday mornings. A few years ago I ran across those forgettable sermons from the Summer of '69. In every seaside homily, regardless of the Scripture, I railed against Richard Nixon and the war.

My poor listeners! Dressed for the beach, dragging rafts, coolers, floats, and flippers, their one week of vacation, pausing on their way to the strand to speak with God, subjected to my tirades. To my mind, my verbal assault upon Tricky Dick certified me as a genuine "prophet." More likely, it assuaged my anger at God for messing with my future by making me be a pastor. In short, my sermons arose, not from my exegesis of a text, but from my sin.

In hortatory sermons I say, "Hey, here's how I cured myself of racism. May I help you with yours?" My efforts to convict and cure them of their sin display my own turpitude. Though Paul told First Church Rome, "All have sinned and fall short of God's glory" (Romans 3:23), when he speaks to Timothy of sin, Paul notes his own, in the present tense: *Christ Jesus came into the world to save sinners—and I'm the biggest sinner of all* (1 Timothy 1:15).

In 1963, eight Alabama clergy (including one of my episcopal predecessors), white liberals all, casting themselves as peacemakers and reconcilers, wrote to Martin Luther King. While in favor of racial justice, they were troubled by the disruption that King's followers were causing Birmingham. They implored King to be more patient and not endanger innocent lives. What you preach is true, it's just that it's inconvenient and out of season.

From his cell in Birmingham jail, King wrote in the spirit of First and Second Timothy, reminding his fellow clergy that their peace could be a cover for cowardice (Paul accuses the elders at Ephesus of "a spirit of cowardice," 2 Timothy 1:7 NRSVue) and sinful accommodation to the powers that be. King kicking butt for Jesus, stirring the pot.

A mimeographed copy of the letter, sent to the city's clergy that week, adorned my episcopal office in Bombingham. King's letter on my wall served as a potent reminder that powerful, privileged bishops always hope that it's possible to follow Jesus without trouble.

I'm troubled that Paul advised the enslaved members of Timothy's churches not be too bothered by their enslavement, even to fellow Christians: Those who are under the bondage of slavery should consider their own masters as worthy of full respect so that God's name and our teaching won't get a bad reputation. And those who have masters who are believers shouldn't look down on them because they are brothers. Instead, they should serve them more faithfully, because the people who benefit from your good service are believers who are loved (1 Timothy 6:1-2). In his concern for the sensibilities of masters, is Paul a precursor of the peacemaking clergy to whom King's letter was addressed?

Paul's belligerent letters are part of the two millennia of argumentation ignited by asking, "If Jesus Christ is the truth about God, how then shall we live? We need to talk."

Hey, separating Global Methodists, ponder that though all of Paul's letters are full of conflicted argument, never, ever does he say, "Therefore, since I can't convince you, we're leaving" much less, "This congregation would be better off if you would leave." Think about it.

Thank God a score of African American Methodists refused to dismiss me with, "We know his family; God will never change his mind."

Leadership Lessons

Because pastors must also be leaders, trouble is unavoidable. Leaders are needed only if an organization must go somewhere (Matthew 28). No leadership required if everyone is walking in the same direction. Trouble is, people reward their pastors for preserving the status quo and punish them for making them uncomfortable by stirring the pot.

From the work of Ron Heifetz I learned that leaders make people uneasy by focusing the organization on problems that the institution has ignored for decades, using its best resources to avoid the pain. Leaders risk saying things that the group would rather left unsaid and then curate the arguments that are sure to follow. Pastors hazard the discomfort in faith that Christ will give his church the resources required to be honest about and then creatively to solve, its problems.

In *The Practice of Adaptive Leadership*, Heifetz says that the adaptive leader can always expect conflict between the values people say they hold and the reality they face. Rather than suppress conflict, the adaptive leader is courageous enough sometimes to instigate, always to orchestrate conflict so that people may begin to envision new ways of thinking and acting.

The body of Christ has never faced the truth and bravely attempted to be faithful to the demands of Jesus without conflict and pushback: Why weren't we told? You are too critical. Who are you to say? If you really loved us, you wouldn't talk like that. Can't we just agree to disagree? We've never done it that way. Let's talk about what's right with this church, not what's wrong. This isn't the right time. Change don't come overnight. The church ain't a business. Where's the grace? There's no way that a little church like ours will be able to. . . . Let us pray.

When you hear comments like these, you'll know you're on the right track, offering a congregation the chance to become the body of Christ in motion.

The main reason the church requires leaders is Christological: Jesus Christ has assigned his mission to the church. Somebody must be called up to convene, equip, train, negotiate, motivate, and send. That's you.

Some leadership advice, even from one so insightful as Heifetz or Rabbi Friedman (whose *A Failure of Nerve* rescued me in three brouhahas as Bishop-in-Bama), sounds managerial and utilitarian, when, as we've said, the only good reasons for leading a church are theological. The best justification for having a church fight is troublemaker Jesus. Never be contentious unless Jesus puts you up to it.

How many congregations are one fierce argument away from having a future? A happy church could be a church that's given up, a congregation that's degenerated into a like-minded alliance of older adults, a blue, red, or purple political rally rather than a mission outpost for the world's true sovereign in a warring world. If so, God's got nobody to stir the pot but you.

I ask my Introduction to Ordained Leadership class, "What will be your greatest ethical challenge as a pastor?" Their most frequent response? "I'm a people pleaser."

There's much that these novices don't know. But if they know that managing conflict will be their chief challenge, they know a great deal.

Thank God I got to enter ministry in a time and place where early on I learned that there are moments when we've got to say more than, "Well, that's your opinion; let's just agree to disagree." Sometimes a desire for your church to be a "big tent," or "keep everyone at the table," is due to a latitudinarian timidity to engage about the doctrine you're supposed to be defending. Jesus warned; he brings peace, but not as the world gives (John 14:27), turning mother against daughter and casting fire on the earth (Luke 12:49-52).

"Easier to put out a fire than to raise the dead," consoled the district superintendent as he assigned me to a church with a reputation for disputation.

From whence does pastoral courage amid conflict arise? An abiding conviction that the gospel not only makes sense but that it is true. An unshakable faith that Jesus Christ wants us to succeed at being his body, his bride, an abiding trust that God will get back what belongs to God. In other words, don't start an argument unless Jesus has egged you on.

Isn't it revealing that I can tell you who has walked because of disagreement with something that I've said in a sermon? How many more just stopped coming, having given up hope that I will say anything of substance to stir their languid spirits?

Got That Wrong

I've begun each chapter with confession that ministry changed my mind about matters that I once thought I knew for sure. How many more conversions will God work in me? My mind awaits a fellow

Christian like you to begin an argument and convince me of my error. Still, no matter how bold you are in confronting me, at the Last Judgment, I fully expect to hear the King say, "Though you meant well at the time, sorry, wish you had done otherwise. You got that one wrong."

Throughout this book I've commended Paul's teaching of Timothy as a model for how to think about ministry to and with God's people. Now I come to matters on which Paul's thought is less than commendable.

"You're writing a book on First Timothy as a treatise on ministry? Even the parts where Paul goes off script on women and slaves?" asked one of my friends who is no friend of Paul's letters to Timothy.

What are we to do with Paul's unhelpful, even hurtful, comments on women? I bring this up in the hope that you and I will learn better to handle our own indefensible prejudices.

Paul, who boasted of his singleness (1 Corinthians 7:7), takes it upon himself to tell congregants how they should be married:

A wife should learn quietly with complete submission. I don't allow a wife to teach or to control her husband. Instead, she should be a quiet listener. Adam was formed first, and then Eve. Adam wasn't deceived, but rather his wife became the one who stepped over the line because she was completely deceived. But a wife will be brought safely through childbirth, if they both continue in faith, love, and holiness, together with self-control (1 Timothy 2:11-15).

Eschatologically worked up Paul, who told the Corinthians, "The time [is] short. From now on, those who have wives should be like people who don't have them. . . . this world . . . is passing away" (1 Corinthians 7:29, 31), now sets up shop as marriage counselor. Throughout his correspondence, Paul is no fan of male-female marriage, scoffing that marriage is for those who burn with lust and can't contain themselves (1 Corinthians 7:9). So now he's an expert on matrimony?

Mr. Salvation by Faith Alone writes that a woman will *be brought safely through childbirth* on the condition that husband and wife *continue in faith, love, and holiness, together with self-control* (2 Timothy 2:15)? I know we're all guilty of theological inconsistencies but, really Paul?

Paul approved of women praying and prophesying (1 Corinthians 11:5, 13; Romans 16), and eloquently sang that there's neither male nor female in Galatians 3:28. But in First Timothy 2:12, Paul contends that wives should be quiet listeners (or worse, 1 Corinthians 14:33b-36, urges women's silence in church). No wonder that many think there's no way the historical Paul could have written these letters.

Maybe Paul is concerned about particular women in a specific situation at Ephesus. If so, I wish he had said not "women" but "that woman." Maybe he is offering a ruling on some troubled, troubling personalities in the congregation and not a general principle applicable to all. (The Jerusalem Council found a way to have kosher rules apply to some but not all in Acts 15:29.)

Above all, Paul's remarks on feminine silence don't make sense when laid alongside the ministry of Christ himself and, as we've said, this faith is all about Christ and our never finished reckoning with his radical, radiant salvation of all. While we are busy interpreting Paul, Jesus actively interprets our interpretation.

Though submission is an unpopular word in our culture, Paul frequently asserts that to be a Christian is, in countless ways, to submit to Christ, and others, in order to be free from the wiles of the world. Trouble is, it sounds like Paul here urges submission only for the women in the congregation. *Complete submission* to *husbands* sounds like women are being asked to be idolaters of their lordly husbands. We all know what the First Commandment thinks of that.

Betty Achtemeier first helped me to see that maybe Paul is addressing a problem among some specific women in the Ephesian congregations who are learning to step out of the traditional roles assigned to them by Gentile male authority and are now taking responsibility for leadership in the church, speaking up and speaking out for Christ. Perhaps some in the church don't like what these newly empowered women are saying. Still, if the church and the gospel had not liberated these women, compelling them to lead by speaking up and speaking out, Paul wouldn't have had a problem to be addressed.

In the temple of multibreasted Artemis of the Ephesians, all the priests were women. Is Paul attempting to characterize the difference between Israel and the church's expectations for women's leadership and that of the pagans? If so, he fumbles the ball.

True, Paul's remarks may be an expression of typical, predictable, patriarchal hierarchy at work. Paul mouthing cultural cliché as if it were the gospel truth. However, they can also be read as wrestling with the newfound implications of the gospel as they pertain to the liberation of everybody in this new, countercultural community called church. Having assured these women in their baptism that they are full participants in the body of Christ, having urged them to follow the leadings of the Holy Spirit and to exercise the gifts of the Spirit, maybe it's just more Spirit-induced freedom of speech than many of the men, including Paul, can handle.

How much of these letters are general, enduing principles for the church and which statements are one-time-only arguments that may have had contextual relevance back then but not here, now?

Context is crucial. I once had a dispute with an associate minister. In my judgment, she had overreached and had said some things in her sermon that did not represent the faith of the church, or the best interests of this congregation. During our discussion, I might've said, "I think you damaged your relationship with people. I urge you not to say it like that again."

If you had walked in on our conversation, you might have thought, "I just heard the senior pastor tell the associate to keep her mouth shut and not talk about controversial things from the pulpit."

You might have also speculated, "I guess our senior pastor is no fan of women preachers." If you thought any of that, you would have been wrong.

Not long ago I ran across a sermon in which I defended the Christian account of marriage. Concerned about the attitudes of my college student congregation, I sought to defend the promises of marriage. To have taken my sermon out of context, as an argument against same-sex unions, would have been an abuse of my sermon.

It's also possible that in my sermon I unintentionally came up with a defense of the theological validity of same-sex unions since I stressed that the church traditionally had little interest in sex or gender; our main concern was fidelity, keeping the promises of marriage, regardless of gender.

Although people picking up a transcript of my sermon later might have interpreted my sermon, in the light of present arguments, as a put down of same-sex unions, my sermon could be read as a defense of such unions, preaching beyond myself, saying more than I was aware of at the time.

Because we know nothing of the specific context of Paul's remarks, perhaps in First Timothy we're watching a pastor react to a congregational conflagration. Paul thinks he needs to exercise a firm hand to put out the fire. This isn't a time for leisurely, give-and-take discussion; let's have a ruling from the chair.

We may grieve at Paul's missed opportunity to take his own words about the radically new salvation in Christ more seriously (as he did in Galatians 3:28). Seems like he simply assumes conventional structures of behavior of women and men and thereby finds himself unintentionally and unconsciously pushing against the implications of the gospel that he has preached. Is that why he doesn't bring up the need for quiescent women in his second letter?

I won't bore you with instances in my ministry when I have been similarly guilty of an inability to live out the implications of the gospel I preached. There's the defeat of the interracial day care center proposal that I should have more doggedly defended. Also the raise that my district superintendents gave themselves that I, as bishop, should have more adamantly opposed. The talented, but controversial young pastor whose appointment to a church I should have pushed, no matter the cost to my prestige. The couple to whom I should have said, "No," but didn't because I feared loss of my relationship with them.

Need I go on?

I want women to enhance their appearance with clothing that is modest and sensible, not with elaborate hairstyles, gold, pearls, or expensive clothes. They should make themselves attractive by doing good, which is appropriate for women who claim to honor God (1 Timothy 2:9-10). Though a few have tried, it's hard to consider such apostolic ramblings a word straight from the Lord. *I want* suggests to me that Paul is expressing a personal preference, *obiter dicta*, not a word from on high.

Besides, from some of the clergy attire I've seen recently, I'd say that Paul should have spent time talking about the outrageous liturgical dress of some men. At a funeral, shorts and a tie-dyed shirt?

Now in regard to virgins, I have no commandment from the Lord, but I give my opinion as one who by the Lord's mercy is trustworthy (1 Corinthians 7:25). A rare instance of apostolic modesty. Teach me to pray, "Lord, if I've got no direct command from you, enable me to keep my mouth shut."

Paul's words on women are a time-and-culture-bound pastoral attempt to speak the gospel in a time and place, not a theology of marriage and family, or gender and church leadership. They're of no help in deciding the role of women in today's church, but they are a humbling reminder to you and to me of how our own church leadership is always subject to corrigibility.

Sometimes you're not trying to pronounce truth, nor are you focused on leading the mission of Jesus Christ; you just want peace and quiet. Maybe Paul's words about women keeping silent are an ad hoc outburst addressed to a situation in which Paul wishes that somebody, or some group, would stop talking. Paul is buying time, attempting to turn down the heat, placing things in a holding pattern, until he can think of something nicer to say than, "Quiet!"

My own church would have been better off, at our most recent disastrous General Conferences, if some bishop had had the guts to shout, both to insufferably pious Traditionalists and virtue-signaling Progressives, "Enough! Silence!" Silencing might have given the Holy Spirit time to intrude into our deliberations, which, so far as I could see, the Spirit did not.

You've never been in the middle of a church argument and said in desperation, "For the love of God, would y'all shut up!"? Never had an outburst like that? Well, good for you.

I'll admit that none of my defense of Paul's words on the silencing of wives works for what he said about slaves. The one who calls himself "a slave of Christ Jesus" (Romans 1:1) and boasts that he is not enslaved to what people in Ephesus think about him, now tells slaves to accept their enslavement.

Maybe Paul means to say to his enslaved siblings in Christ that even if others regard you as their slave, that's not the way Christ thinks about you, nor should you think that way about yourself:

Those who are under the bondage of slavery should consider their own masters as worthy of full respect so that God's name and our teaching won't get a bad reputation. And those who have masters who are believers shouldn't look down on them because they are brothers. Instead, they should serve them more faithfully, because the people who benefit from your good service are believers who are loved (1 Timothy 6:1-2).

Then, "Were you a slave when you were called? Don't let it trouble you—although if you can gain your freedom, do so" (1 Corinthians 7:21).

I'm glad that Paul at least said *although if you can gain your freedom, do so.* He preached that nobody should be a slave in Galatians 5:1, even to God's Torah. Why didn't Paul say that here?

I'll grant that Paul could not have imagined a world without slavery, or without emperors, and it was unimaginable that anybody in the Ephesus congregation could subvert either of these institutions. Paul neither defended nor condemned Roman slavery, but in these passages simply names slavery as part of life and then attempts to imagine how slavery could be lived under Jesus Christ.

Still, Paul must answer, as must we all, to Christ. Jesus is Lord, Lord over all social arrangements. Maybe it took a while for Paul to come to a Galatians 3:23 understanding of women in the church. If so, Paul took less time than it took for white, somewhat enlightened, sort of democratic, mostly Christian America to admit that our notions of African slavery were wrong. Even longer, a lot longer, for us to attempt to do something about it. It would be cheap of me to overlook the injustices still perpetrated against the great-great-grandchildren of enslaved African Americans with, "At least we no longer defend slavery, unlike Paul."

Maybe what's amazing is that, even in Paul's culture and time-bound imagination, he could imagine a world in which the enslaved were regarded as full human beings, beloved by God, responsible moral agents, bodily present in the congregation, subjects of care, instruction, and equal communicants of the Lord's body and blood.

Where slave and free worshipped Christ together, the congregation was pioneering new social arrangements, even more remarkable than the church itself understood. Those whom the world designated as master and slave, Paul now calls siblings in Christ.

I take comfort that someone who was so dramatically called by Christ, a brother with a mind better than mine, was in important ways a child of his age, a brilliant thinker who was capable of falling prey to the wisdom of the world. How great it would be, in current church fights, if more of us could say, "On this subject, I could be as wrong as Saint Paul about slavery."

As somebody who has been in the trenches with Jesus, in the thick and thin of church life, down and dirty with the baptized, I feel about as close to Paul, *biggest sinner of them all*, in these passages as anywhere in his letters to Timothy.

You know that I love Karl Barth, but Barth's (thankfully, few) comments on men and women make me quail (*Church Dogmatics*, III, 2).[1] Surely Barth would now flinch at how some have used him to bolster their bogus notion of "complementarianism." Still, I take heart, when

125

confronted by my own theological gaffs, that if one so great as Barth could be wrong, it's unsurprising that I can be too.

Contending with Contentious Scripture

Paul doles out instructions for dealing with young and old men and women, widows, and slaves. Some of this is not Paul's best work. Still, reading these sections of his letter may be instructive, not in how to treat women or the enslaved, but in how to deal with Scripture.

In First Timothy 5:3-8 there's an uncomfortable moment when Paul dares to distinguish between deserving destitute widows and those less deserving with words about widows that are about as tough as he dispenses upon the rich (1 Timothy 6:17-19). I've spent my ministry battling any attempt by church people to sort out the poor between the deserving and undeserving. What are we to make of Paul doing just that?

> *Take care of widows who are truly needy. . . . A widow who is truly needy and all alone puts her hope in God and keeps on going with requests and prayers, night and day. But a widow who tries to live a life of luxury is dead even while she is alive. . . . Put a widow on the list who is older than 60 years old and who was faithful to her husband. She should have a reputation for doing good: raising children, providing hospitality to strangers, washing the feet of the saints, helping those in distress, and dedicating herself to every kind of good thing. But don't accept younger widows for the list. When their physical desires distract them from Christ, they will want to get married. Then they will be judged for setting aside their earlier commitment. Also, they learn to be lazy by going from house to house. They are not only lazy but they also become gossips and busybodies, talking about things they shouldn't. So I want younger widows to marry, have children, and manage their homes so that they won't give the enemy any reason to slander us. (Some have already turned away to follow Satan.) If any woman who is a believer has widows in her family, she*

should take care of them and not burden the church, so that it can help other widows who are truly needy. (1 Timothy 5:3, 5-6, 9-16)

Surprising that not all widows were impoverished and in need of food and money (1 Timothy 5:6). I would have thought widowhood, in that time and place, would have condemned a woman to live out the rest of her days in desperate need. That Paul can say that some widows were not destitute may be testimonial to the pluck of these Christian women who believed the promises made to them in their baptism. Maybe the church had done a good job of empowering those who would otherwise be desperate, telling them that, even in their widowhood, they have resources *and* a vocation to use what they have in caring for others.

If some of these widows were poor, and if they were old, I'm impressed that Paul tells them that doesn't disqualify them from service and leadership, *raising children, providing hospitality to strangers, washing the feet of the saints, helping those in distress,* and dedicating themselves *to every kind of good thing* (1 Timothy 5:10). These widows, even in misfortune, are persons with agency who are under vocational obligation to use what they have for the good of others. To help people in need who were not part of your biological family would have been a strange, politically subversive idea in Greco-Roman culture.

I also understand that a congregation that steps up and shoulders financial responsibility for those in need must be prepared for tough decisions about how congregational resources are used. Never had a church fight over just who we'll take responsibility to help and who we won't? Ever boasted, "Money is never a problem in this church"? Sounds like a congregation that has a limited view of its missional responsibilities.

Take care of widows who are truly needy (1 Timothy 5:3). I was the young associate minister, so the senior pastor expected me (who else?) tirelessly to visit "shut-ins," as we used to call the elderly homebound.

Most were widows. All pled home confinement as the reason church should come to them rather than their coming to church.

I discovered that for some, homebound didn't prohibit trips to the Caribbean or shopping jaunts to the big city. I was being enlisted by older adults to undergird their delusion that age exempted them from responsibility for anybody but themselves.

"There's no retirement from the vocation of discipleship," I lectured, whenever I could catch them between cruises.

If you spend much of your ministry in mainline Protestantism, you will mostly be around people my age. The best care for those of us over sixty is to encourage the social interaction that occurs through active participation in the life of the congregation and to help us as their Christians find our God-given ministries, *raising children, providing hospitality to strangers, washing the feet of the saints, helping those in distress.* My model is reformer John Calvin who, at his end, asked to be propped on pillows and a book placed in his aged hands saying, "Would you have God come and find me idle?"[2]

Stay away from the godless myths that are passed down from the older women (1 Timothy 4:7), Paul's occasionally sexist, ageist stereotypes on display. Still, while I'll always be indebted to my dear grandmother for the wisdom she imparted (just like Timothy's grandmother, Lois) each day after school with milk and cookies, thank God that Jesus insisted I discard her *godless myths* about the faded glories of the Old South.

When Paul extols the virtues of motherhood and childbearing, the challenges of parenting and clothing, he blesses the quotidian, here and now of the Christian life, and sanctifies the mundane, domestic, and ordinary. Although I squirm at some of nonparent Paul's parental advice, in these letters so consumed with intra-ecclesial concerns, by commenting on families, Paul ennobles the everyday submission to the needs of children and the aged, which is the heroic, sacrificial vocation of many Christians.

In a culture of loneliness and fragmentation, the time and energy that we clergy give to mundane matters like marriage, family, and the nurture of children, becomes a witness to our people that the Christian life must be lived right here and now.

Say hello to Prisca and Aquila and the household of Onesiphorus. . . . Try hard to come to me before winter. Eubulus, Pudens, Linus, Claudia, and all the brothers and sisters say hello. The Lord be with your spirit. Grace be with you all (1 Timothy 4:19, 21-22).

Questions from pastor Gabby Cudjoe Wilkes. Gabby and her husband, Andrew, founded The Double Love Experience Church in Brooklyn, New York. They are the authors of *Psalms for Black Lives: Reflections for the Work of Liberation.*

1. Pot-stirrers are instigators. Growing up, instigators were frowned upon. Here's my question: Aren't leaders called to do more than stir the pot but to also support folks as a stirred pot brings up areas of disagreement?

2. I appreciate the sociocultural context provided for Paul in this chapter. How do we surface those kinds of conditions for the everyday Bible reader?

3. How do we balance preaching truth to power (as you did about Nixon and the Vietnam War) and preaching hope for congregants' personal issues?

HEARING AND SPEAKING GOD'S WORD

Some passages of Scripture cause friction until a preacher, through explication, makes them less troubling.

The Bible is a human product bound to a time and place in history. Preachers must perform laborious separation of what's human, historical, and contingent from what's spiritual, eternal, and relevant in order for a biblical text to speak.

Although I've been called to be a preacher, I'm still just one of the guys attempting to share some helpful spiritual insights from my experience.

What a relief to discover, in my first days, that I had reasonably good people skills that could be used to good effect as pastor.

"Admit it, you were wrong," I said to my mother as I ended my first year unscathed. "People like me."

I had yet to learn that ministry was not about me.

Preaching God's Word

Karl Barth taught that the one Word of God reiterates and self-reveals in three ways: Christ, eternal Logos, the unique, bodily present Word; Scripture, the word of God remembered, recorded; and, of all things, preaching, God's word here, now, heard and then spoken by preachers like us.[1]

The laity, hearing the Protestant Reformers' assertion that the preached word is none other than God's speech, may think that we clergy are flattered that our humble words can be God's. How little they know.

Paul is clear that church is a challenge, preaching and mission are demanding, and Christian leadership is not for the faint of heart because it's all at the behest of the One who was revealed as a human, declared righteous by the Spirit, seen by angels, preached throughout the nations, believed in around the world, and taken up in glory (1 Timothy 3:16). If Jesus had not complicated our notions of God by not only being revealed as a human but also by being taken up in glory, I wouldn't need to struggle giving advice nor would you need to read this book.

On Sundays when Scripture is read, the reader says, "The word of the Lord, for the people of God." The congregation responds gleefully, "Thanks be to God." Some of them are lying.

Jesus's favorite prophet, Isaiah, displays what it's like to speak up for a God who incarnates, not only into our flesh, but also in human language,

> The LORD God gave me an educated tongue
> to know how to respond to the weary
> with a word that will awaken them in the morning.
> God awakens my ear in the morning to listen,
> as educated people do. (Isaiah 50:4)

Like Isaiah, we empty-handed preachers must be "educated" by the gift of the Lord's word; we preach what we've been told. Our counsel, care, and proclamation stand under the judgment of the Lord who "responds to the weary" by jolting them awake. To rouse the somnambulant, prophets must be given awakened ears and the guts to say what we've heard.

Why am I ambivalent about the significance of my own preaching? I doubt it's due to my humility. More likely, I am reluctant to take responsibility for the power of God working on me, in spite of me, for purposes beyond me. It's unnerving. Though I construct a sermon, I cannot control or delimit the disruptive fecundity of the Word.

Just like Isaiah.

We moderns expect no messages except the self-generated. To hear God's "external word" (Luther) requires reeducation. The news for which we're listening is so countercultural and counterintuitive that there's no way to hear it except as gift. Thus, the prophet says, "The LORD God opened my ear; / I didn't rebel; I didn't turn my back" (Isaiah 50:5).

In twenty treks through the three-year Common Lectionary, how often has my ear been opened to a word that I would never have come up with on my own. Alas, how often has that word seemed so odd or inconvenient to speak, that I laid it aside and preached instead from my own experience or theirs, a safer word than the Lord's. Unlike Isaiah, I did "rebel" and "turn my back" upon God's peculiar speech.

Why had I the need to protect God's people from the assault of God's self-disclosure? After all, it was they who asked, by their presence, "Is there a word from the LORD?" (Jeremiah 37:17). You may remember that it was King Zedekiah, trembling at his enemy's approach, who carelessly sought consolation from a preacher, "Got a word from the Lord?"

"Sure," said Jeremiah. "You're going to be handed over to the king of Babylon." Can't say King Z didn't ask for it.

Why did I, unlike Isaiah, rebel and turn my back? I'll explain. Look what Isaiah got for speaking the word he heard:

> I gave my body to attackers,
>   and my cheeks to beard pluckers.
> I didn't hide my face
>   from insults and spitting. (Isaiah 50:6)

Jesus, the Word, came practicing and preaching God's word and got his beard plucked, spit in his face, even worse.

Piero della Francesca, Flagellation of Christ (1468–1470)

See Christ whipped as three elegantly dressed bigwigs calmly discuss some business matter in a geometrically balanced Roman palace courtyard. Pilate rests comfortable upon his judgment seat as the Son of God is tortured within an inch of his life. Christ is bound to a classical column topped off with a golden godlet. Everything is serene, decent, and well-law-and-ordered. Christ has spoken and now the world talks back.

Forever thereafter, when we speak of "God" we must refer to the somber truth depicted in this painting. Jesus was crucified in a vain attempt to shut him up.

"God as Jesus Christ? Jesus Christ as God? We won't stand for it," we cried in unison. After an empathetic sigh, we went back to business as usual.

Only to have him show back up among us, even us. "As I was saying before I was so rudely interrupted . . ."

Scripture

Scripture is a major way that God preserves us from making "God" mean whatever we want. God not only became flesh, showing up bodily, physically, in history, Jesus also preached. We said we wanted to hear from God. God spoke: *Jesus Christ,* the unexpected (and in many ways, unwanted) God Almighty who is also the human who "gave my body to attackers, / and my cheeks to beard pluckers" and "didn't hide my face / from insults and spitting" (Isaiah 50:6).

Equally outrageous, that same crucified/resurrected God/human chose to save the world by summoning humans like us, Jeremiah, Isaiah, and Mary to turn our backs on the world in order to contend for God's love of the world and to tell the world all about it. Scripture: Revelation borne on our frail, finite human backs, exposing us to the spitting and insults that often arise when God's external word is read and preached.

In claiming that both Scripture and preaching can be God's word, we make the astounding claim that God graciously gives God's Word—but not without human help. Look at us, finding revelation in a couple of letters written to Timothy two thousand years ago. Why be surprised that God may speak even through your sermon next Sunday?

It takes three to make sense of Scripture: one to read and interpret (me), another to argue and wrestle with a fellow Christian's interpretation (you), and God to show up and speak to the both of us (the Holy

Spirit). Therefore, if we want to hear and then preach First and Second Timothy, we must pray, "Come on Holy Spirit, make these ancient human words your word to contemporary human us."

Scripture resists easy, knock-down, sure-fire explication. Time and again, in my biblical study, a passage has broken free of my grasp, turned on me, recanted what I thought I had earlier heard, sending me away empty-handed or else giving me more than I bargained for. We call it a "passage" of Scripture, God's word active, moving sometimes away, sometimes toward us, passing free of our grip, just like God.

I've heard some evangelicals speak of Scripture being "absolute truth." By talking in this modern way I guess they try to bolster the Bible against the ravages of contemporary moral "relativism." They are wrong. In the Christian faith, there's no freestanding, detached, absolute anything. All is relative to and utterly dependent upon the risen Christ to show up and make it true for us.

For instance, though it's tough to know what Paul is getting at in his very few, debatable comments on sexual relations between people of the same gender, Paul is as unequivocal as our Lord in condemnation of heterosexual divorce and remarriage. "To the married I give this command—not I, but the Lord—that the wife should not separate from her husband (but if she does separate, let her remain unmarried or else be reconciled to her husband) and that the husband should not divorce his wife" (1 Corinthians 7:10-11). Period.

"Not I, but the Lord," Paul at his most absolute.

Of course, it's been a long time since my wing of the church has taken Paul's comments on divorce, much less Jesus's, authoritatively as "God's word" abstracted from the pastoral care of actual Christians in real congregations. That's as it should be. Scripture is a word from Jesus to Jesus's people, the church, in the Spirit of Jesus. Everything, especially Scripture, is relative to Jesus and his mission.

I'm told that at a recent meeting of the breakaway, misnamed Global Methodist Church, as they sat around backslapping themselves on how seriously they took the "authority of Scripture" (except

Scripture's prohibitions against eating pork, shellfish, or remarriage after divorce), celebrating their unquestioning obedience to Scripture's straightforward (to them) condemnation of all matters LGBTQ+, somebody said, "When are we going to take Scripture seriously in its prohibition on women preaching?"

Oops.

Not to beat up on the many GMC leaders who divorced and remarried, I just wish they would stop justifying their positions on sexual orientation with Paul's offhand, "It seems right to me . . ." comments and instead ask themselves the rudimentary, but utterly appropriate, Christological WDJD, "What Did Jesus Do?"

Is it not enough that Paul tells Christian leaders like us not to be *greedy* but also to see that our *children are obedient with complete respect*, sneering *if they don't know how to manage their own household, how can they take care of God's church?* (1 Timothy 3:3-5). Considering my household managerial shortcomings, my consolation is that Paul's offhanded comments on child management come from one who knew nothing firsthand of marriage or teenaged children.

Chalcedonian Imagination

The theological rationale for Paul's expending so much energy, in a church letter, on domestic matters and nuts-and-bolts intramural congregational squabbles, wasn't carefully thought out until long after Paul. The Council of Chalcedon (451 C.E., in your faded Church History 101 notes, look it up) helped the church to think incarnationally, that is paradoxically, about Jesus Christ and, by implication, about anything Christ is mixed up with. The Definition of Chalcedon delineated the orthodoxy of Nicea with the seemingly puzzling affirmation of the wonder of Christ's humanity and divinity united in one person, yet divinity and humanity never confused, mixed, separated or detached. Christ, unreservedly divine and, in the same person, fully, completely human.

Our Lord Jesus Christ, the same perfect in Godhead and also perfect in manhood; truly God and truly man . . . in all things like unto us, without sin; begotten before all ages of the Father, . . . for us and for our salvation, born of the Virgin Mary, the Mother of God, . . . one and the same Christ, Son, Lord, only begotten, to be acknowledged in two natures, inconfusedly, unchangeably, indivisibly, inseparably; the distinction of natures being by no means taken away by the union, . . . as the prophets from the beginning declared concerning Him, and the Lord Jesus Christ Himself has taught us, and the Creed of the holy Fathers has handed down to us.

Sure, the church could have said it more simply than Nicaea but if we had, we wouldn't have been talking about Christ as presented in Scripture. Christ's two natures, unified in one person (*hypostasis*) yet neither confused, mixed, nor separated and detached. Christ entirely, unreservedly divine and, in the same person, Christ fully, completely human.

Karl Barth taught me to use "Chalcedonian imagination" (as Deborah and George Hunsinger call it) not only for thinking about Christ, but also to ministry.[2] To keep in Chalcedonian harmony and tension, the utterly human and at the same time, truly godly practice of Christian ministry insures that pastoral work will be as difficult and demanding, and as adventurous and astonishing as an incarnate God intends ministry to be.

In all acts of ministry, not only in preaching, God unashamedly solicits and enables human participation in God's love for and deployment of God's people. Nothing in ministry is immaculately conceived; it's so human. At the same time, nothing good occurs that is not partnered with God. A living, intervening God makes our human acts mean more than we can make them mean. God loves God's world by miraculously speaking to God's world through frail, finite preachers like us.

We're not free to limit our ministry only to what can be humanly accomplished—a happy, content congregation, reasonably upbeat congregants, more-or-less comprehensible sermons, a repaved church parking lot, a new stove for the church kitchen. Nor can we attempt to defuse a passage of Scripture into an inert, passive, ancient text. It's Scripture, a speaking presence discontent to convey history or spiritual ideas; it wants your soul.

At the same time, we have no reason to think that God will save the world without utilizing frail, finite creatures like us. Just as Chalcedon keeps us from cutting God down to our manageability, so it guards against reducing ministry to our control. God condescends to use us to do God's work (vocation), and yet God's work is not done as we please, void of divine instigation, intervention, correction, and incarnation. So in this book I can't say simply, "Look at me; I changed my mind," but my long, boney finger must point, "Look at God through whom my mind has been changed."

Just as biblical texts are words that the church has complexified by discovering them as Holy Scripture, so you, as a human being on whose head hands have been laid, when urged to "Just be yourself," or "Take care of yourself" can justifiably respond, "My self has been complicated by vocation."

Take pastoral comfort in Chalcedon. From all eternity, God has elected to turn toward us, self-binding with us, choosing not to be God without us, not to rule in heaven alone; in the Incarnation, becoming one of us yet not dependent upon nor determined by us. When God declared, "I will be your God; you will be my people," God meant it. Whenever God's word is heard, as God's word, through one of my fumbling sermons, whenever some hurting human life is encountered by God's healing power in my modest acts of pastoral care, if eyes are opened and somebody sees God even in my turgid teaching, it's an everyday, mundane demonstration of God's decisive, eternal turning toward us, "for us and for our salvation," evidence that Chalcedon's claims for the fully-human-fully-God Christ are true. God wants fellowship with frail, flawed, fickle humanity. And yet God also wants more out of us than our finite humanity can generate on our own.

As pastors, it's not our job to get them all scrubbed up and ready to meet their Maker. Christ has already come out to meet them as they are, showing up as the One who got into trouble for partying with the likes of them, the Messiah who paid dearly for never turning any sinner away, the Savior who saved those whom nobody thought could be saved, or wanted saved.

Troubled Texts

"All of these new things are from God, who reconciled us to himself through Christ . . . by not counting people's sins against them. He has trusted us with this message of reconciliation" (2 Corinthians 5:18-19). Period. Barth said that these words of Paul are the whole of the good news: Our relationship with God is totally initiated and sustained by God who has freely determined from all eternity to have us and then, wonder of wonders, God "trusted us with this message of reconciliation" (v. 19). If anybody meets Jesus, it's through thoroughly human us, having heard news from the human/divine Bible and then passed on what we've heard.

When dealing with human-divine biblical texts, I had to learn that a troubling passage is not a hindrance to interpretation and preaching but rather a God-given invitation. I began ministry thinking of Scripture as an obstacle that I had to work around, deconstruct (or maybe dispose of) in order for Scripture to speak to contemporary, thoughtful, critically thinking moderns, like the people I wished were in my church. I had either to meet the demands of the world in front of the text (today's church) or had to learn enough historical criticism and linguistic expertise to reconstruct the world behind the text (the originating historical context) in order to make sense of the text.

Then ministry changed my mind. In the weekly struggle with the biblical text ("Speak! I've got less than twenty-four hours before I'm in the pulpit!") I learned to look for the weird, to embrace troublesome-ness as a valuable interpretive door into the text: Why does this text say so little about matters that I care about so much? Why did the master of the house become violently angry when his little one-talent-servant prudently buried his talent? What made the congregation at Nazareth go nuts when Jesus preached? Does Paul neither know nor care about Jesus's birth? Walking on water? Never seen that in Greenville. Surely he didn't say, "Hate your mother." Jesus on a bad day?

The Holy Spirit taught me that a biblical text's quirkiness, dissonance, paradox, and trouble are a preacher's friends. Obvious truth may be true, but it's rarely interesting. When we read a biblical passage with a Chalcedonian imagination, we apply our human minds, under the influence of the One who entrusted to us the news of Christ's accomplishment of our reconciliation, to a human text that means to be more than human. You go to the text hoping for a surprise. Then you announce that surprise from the pulpit, enjoying those congregants who are surprised.

Only a Chalcedonian imagination makes sense of the claim that Scripture, like Paul's letters to Timothy, can be both an utterly human word—spoken to real people in this world, sometimes unhelpful, routinely domesticated, even trivial, in places, dead wrong—that is also an address from God so odd and wonderful, so opposed to us in order to save us, that there's no way it could have originated with us.

It's okay to assert "the authority of Scripture" but the moment you relax the Chalcedonian paradox and lapse into the unorthodox boast that the Bible is pristine, divine speaking apart from the human voice, you've claimed too little.

Scripture is theanthropic. More than a deposit of divine wisdom, report on what God once said, it's dynamic address by a living God who refuses to be apophatic when it comes to communion with humanity. In the same action, Scripture is God electing to communicate with us through people, and sometimes saying things through Paul that are more than Paul meant to say that have relevance beyond the time and place of Paul.

Because God Incarnate is Jesus Christ, there's no way to meet God untainted by the human and no way to be human apart from God's relentless intent to be in communion with humanity, assigning us roles to play in God's reconciling mission.

By the grace of God, I've had stunning moments when I paused, as I was muddling through leadership of Sunday worship, and pondered the wonder of a congregation assembled before utterly human me (so full of contradictions and errors) in order to submit to an utterly human, ancient text (renowned for its inconsistencies and ambiguities) in the hope they'll be reconciled to God. Even though none of them has ever heard of Chalcedon.

In writing to Timothy, then to us, I don't understand why Paul gets so worked up over things that seem to me trivial and inconsequential. Who cares about jewelry or gossip much less the errors of Alexander the Silversmith?

But through the lens of Chalcedon, I'm reminded that we've got a reconciling God who connects with kids, wine, money, politicians, and sex and thereby redeems all human life. As godliness redefined, Jesus Christ has forever made problematic a too rigid separation between spiritual and carnal, human and divine.

There are things I wish Paul hadn't said about women or the enslaved. I can understand why some feel these comments impugn all of Paul's letters. It's then that Chalcedon reminds me that Jesus Christ embraces us as we are, where we are, "for us and for our salvation," upfront about his mission to save sinners, only sinners. Some sin by saying that we don't, as if all that we say is being said by God. Others sin in saying, "I may not be the best Christian in the world but at least I'm too good to say anything as sinful as what Paul said."

I want, in this book, to say what I thought needed to be said to you, in the way I wanted to say it, hoping that you'll hear what I say as I intend. But, from years of speaking for God, I know that what you'll hear is beyond my control. Go ahead. I'm okay if you hear things in this book that caused you to say, "Oh my. I wish he hadn't said that." To which the Lord chimes in, "Amen!"

Any Christian is, according to Luther, *simul justis et peccator,* a sinner subject to Christ's ongoing, justifying work. When my *peccator* gets the best of Christ's *justis,* all I can do is pray *Mea culpa* and be grateful that the One who calls is also the merciful One who judges and forgives.

Barth, citing Kierkegaard, as I recall, said that a good sermon should be like a pane of clear glass that enables the congregation to look through the preacher straight toward God. The metaphor breaks down in light of Chalcedon. In ministry, God doesn't obliterate our humanness but rather commandeers our humanity for God's reconciling work. Just as you can't separate Jesus's humanity from his divinity and still have Jesus who is God Incarnate (the error of those who searched for the "historical Jesus"), so you can't filter out my body, voice, brain, economic location, gender, temperament, or psyche and still have me, the one who, for reasons known only to God, has been called to speak for God.

Ministry, Human and Divine

I left academia and answered the call of my church to the episcopacy partly because I knew that Christ means for his good news to be embodied, incorporated, and put into practice. Could I lead the church to flesh out the ideas I had been teaching?

That's why I admire greatly what you are doing, as a church leader and pastor, in risking the hard, corporate work required to actually be the church, Christ taking up room in your part of the world. I guess I don't need to tell you that your life would have been easier if you had been called by God to get your PhD in Church History and write books about the significance of the Nicean Creed. Instead, you're called to care for the people who are trying to live Nicea's claims in a congregation, together, here, now. Bless you.

Academics have always been embarrassed that, when God appeared in the flesh, it was as a Jew from Nazareth and not as a tenured professor from Cambridge. If you were doing Church History, you could endlessly defer judgment, keep pondering, reflecting, and ruminating in the unchurched solitude of your study. But you are a preacher who must climb into a pulpit and speak next Sunday, announce a verdict, let your ideas go public, so that God's word may take flesh and blood among us, as the Word so chooses.

When we preachers worry about bodily, structural matters like sermon design, form, tone, arrangement, and delivery, we imitate biblical writers. It's not enough to have good ideas; ideas must become enfleshed. Why do the Gospels render their presentations of Jesus as a compendium of travel stories? Why would Paul, in his letters to Timothy, name names, bog down in messy congregational squabbles, begin with flattering salutations and end with earnestly pleading summations? Chalcedonian imagination in action, spirit and flesh, heaven and earth in conversation without either being confused, mixed, separated, or detached.

When we read Scripture we're in the middle of everyday life, real people attempting to adjust themselves to the shock of salvation by a really divine, truly human Jesus. Scripture is the sort of literature you get when human beings like us attempt to talk about the God who, though infinitely not like us, became one with us in order to be in conversation with us.

Bless you as you sit through boring church meetings ("It's 9:30! Can't we vote and go home?"), wander through the halls of an apartment house knocking on bolted doors ("Helen, I know you are in there, and I'm not leaving until you open this door."), waste hours attempting to referee among the volunteers at the soup kitchen ("When she called you an 'incompetent idiot,' I'm sure she didn't mean it like it sounded."), sleep on a dirt floor in a hut in a village in Honduras on the youth mission trip ("Put out that cigar! It's two in the morning!"), and try to raise bail for the kid whose parents have disowned him because of his DUI. You do it in the spirit of the indefinable Lord whom Chalcedon did its best to define.

I'm sure that one of the reasons why I am so much engaged by Paul's epistles is that they are so self-evidently the work of a pastor, attempting to speak God's word amid the tug and pull, scratching and clawing, faithfulness and sin of congregations just like yours. God's Word become flesh, our flesh, tenting with us (John 1:14), not as the saints we wish we were, but as sinners toward whom God has decisively turned, all "for us and for our salvation."

Sometimes reading, teaching, and preaching Scripture, I don't know which side of the Chalcedonian affirmation—Christ fully human, fully divine—is a greater challenge. I'm uncomfortable exposing Saint Paul as someone who is, at least in his remarks about women, culturally bound, a man of his time, so much like me. Paul's snide attacks upon his critics, calling them out by name, telling them to go to hell for all he cares, are some of the most human-all-too-human moments in the New Testament. Thank God nobody canonized any of my sermon flops or post-meeting tantrums.

Honestly though, I'm more unnerved when Paul, languishing in a jail cell awaiting certain execution, bursts into hopeful, hymnic praise for the all-sufficiency of Christ and his triumphant Lordship, all evidence to the contrary. Or Paul, while attempting to speak authoritatively, apostolically for God to Timothy and his congregations, candidly admits that none of them is as big a sinner as the preacher himself. Such hope and truthfulness do not arise from exclusively human sources.

As a preacher, I've a score of human reasons why people don't listen to my sermons. People are distracted, biblically illiterate, obtuse, thick-headed, and worse. Of course they don't hear the word of God, even when it's expertly, eloquently handed to them with three points and a poem.

But when they respond occasionally with, "Your sermon really spoke to me today," or "I was deeply offended by what you said," or "I came here, hoping to receive comfort only to have God give me an outrageous assignment," I discover that my ministry is a volatile, irrepressible, but undeniable Chalcedonian mix of the human endeavor and divine intervention.

"I was really worried, when I entered ministry, that I wouldn't be able to overcome the sexist resistance to women pastors. I discovered that God finds a way. The Lord keeps stepping up and making my ministry work when I doubted it would."

"I can't stand pious, holier-than-thou pastors," he said, not six years into ministry. "So I was determined to keep showing my people that I am one of the guys, just like them. But they insisted on calling me 'Preacher,' even though I asked for 'Steve.' They need a priest, someone who is more than just one of the guys."

We're the ones with the challenging task of standing up and unashamedly proclaiming, "Thus saith the Lord!" *and* also confessing with young Isaiah, "Mourn for me; I'm ruined! I'm a man with unclean lips, and I live among a people with unclean lips" (Isaiah 6:5). We've got to believe that Jesus knew what he was doing when he called frail, finite people like us to be heralds and that Jesus knows how to use our talents (and flaws and foibles) to recover what rightly belongs to him.

While it can be delusional to say, "These are not my words; they are God's word given to me for you," it can also be cowardly to beg off with, "These are just my ideas, suggestions, take or leave them as you will." Feigned humility in the pulpit is often arrogance that refuses to bend one's life in obedience to God's call to serve the Word.

No need to agonize over whether what you said last Sunday was a shabby human rant or a divinely inspired bolt from the blue. You'd be the last to know, right? A human incarnating God shows scant interest in separating the human from the divine.

When we think of Incarnation, Christ assuming our flesh, we're apt to think of his Nativity. Paul never refers to Bethlehem and the manger. In thinking Incarnation, Paul thinks of the Passion, Christ's willing endurance of the world's spitting, beard plucking reaction to his good news and then of his resurrection, God's great "no" to the world's violent, ultimately ineffective "no." "How the high has come so low! How divinity has crept into humanity," marvels Augustine. Jesus may be crucified; but he is also Lord, Prince of Peace, but not as the world gives peace. He calls us to speak, but without guarantees, promising miraculously to give us the right words to say when we stand before the world's tribunals (Mark 13:11), though with the warning that the world may respond to our words as it did to his.

As pastor, teacher, and preacher I'm under orders to "equip God's people" (Ephesians 4:12). Like any pastor, my significance is in how well I give God's people the right words to say when they speak up before a contentious world that prefers the church to keep the truth about God to itself. I goad the faithful to act up before the powers-that-be, letting their light shine so that the world may get a glimpse of Christ through them (Matthew 5:14).

Though my words crack, fade, ricochet off church walls, and die, the Word of the Lord endures forever (Isaiah 48; 1 Peter 1:25). Our long, thin, boney fingers of sermons point beyond ourselves toward Christ as he insists, in his Incarnation, on continuing to self-reveal. Our lives would be easier if he hadn't said some of the things he said and says, still, he speaks. While I wish the Holy Spirit would show up every Sunday between 11:30 and noon, she shows up enough, speaks through me in sufficient sermons to keep me, and the congregation, nervous.

Nail Christ to a cross, seal him in a tomb, dismiss his teaching with a sophisticated sneer, he will, in the power of the Spirit, have the last word.

Screw up my biblical interpretation, sermon DOA, a resurrected Christ is still able to rise up and have his say.

Attempt to shield them from demanding Jesus, rework and explain his good news to make it easier to swallow, use vague, abstract words and cover with spiritual inanities so sweet you could pour it on a waffle, he will insist on tenting among us, bodily present in word, water, wine, and bread, God too close for comfort. Thank God.

Here's how I recounted one such visitation in my memoir, *Accidental Preacher*:

> How I loved Birmingham's Church of the Reconciler—church for, by, and with the homeless. The first time I preached at Church of the Rec, after the Call to Worship, I gazed at the gathering gleaned off the city streets and realized that my proposed sermon was a stupid mistake. I tossed my sermon and prayed, "Come on Lord, give me something. I'm dying down here. You owe me. Line!" That frantic prayer, though prayed often, has rarely been answered—the Lord builds character by having a preacher publicly experience being "poor in spirit." But that day, with a congregation of the wretched of the streets before me, the Holy Spirit fed me the words.
>
> "It's always a blessing to be with you," I began. "Now the question for this morning: What did Jesus do for a living? What line of work was he in?" [Where on earth did I come up with that?]
>
> Silence. Finally someone ventured, "Carpentry?"
>
> "Good guess. No. His daddy Joseph was a carpenter, but no record of Jesus ever helping out in the shop."
>
> "A preacher?" tried another.
>
> "Right! But back then, people didn't yet know that you could defang a preacher with a good salary and a fat pension. No, Jesus couldn't have earned a living wage by preaching."
>
> "Did Jesus have an apartment?" somebody called out.
>
> "Great question!" I said. "Nothing about Jesus working, but we do know that, 'even foxes have holes to crawl into at night but the Son of Man has nowhere to lay his head.'
>
> "Here's the truth: Jesus Christ was an unemployed, homeless, beggar. . . . that's why he accepted so many dinner invitations, even to homes where he wasn't liked. He was hungry and had nowhere else to go."

Somebody down front shouted, "That's alright Jesus! I ain't got no job neither! That's alright!" Applause in the congregation. "That's alright!"

"No job, no house, no nothin' just like Jesus!" shouted a woman who danced in the aisle as the band struck up. General applause and adoration from the assembly.

A few raucous minutes later, I waved the congregation to silence. "You've got my drift. Christians believe that a homeless, (drumroll), jobless ('Amen!') Jew ('Go ahead!') is the whole truth about who God is and what God is up to.

"So," I shouted above the joyful din, "that means that even with degrees from Yale and Emory, even though I can read this stuff in Greek, some of you are closer to Jesus than your bishop!" Dancing and shouting resumed. [Way to go, Holy Spirit.]

As I left Church of the Rec that day in my bishopmobile, the same sister who danced in church was shouting to some men trading smokes under the bridge down the street, "There goes that preacher who has done gone and told us the truth!"[3]

Here's my point: I didn't do that by myself. Holy Spirit, it's a joy to work words with you.

Questions from Lillian Daniel, pastor, teacher, writer, and Michigan Conference Minister of the United Church of Christ. Author (with Martin B. Copenhaver), of *This Odd and Wondrous Calling: The Public and Private Lives of Two Ministers.*

1. Who died and made the three-year Common Lectionary God? In your treks through, ever wonder if the lectionary was created for a biblically literate congregation that most preachers will never encounter? Has the lectionary lost its usefulness? I was taught that the lectionary keeps a pastor from preaching the same texts all the time, but what I

wasn't taught was that the lectionary has biases, in that it skips big chunks of Scripture related to hell and damnation. What do you think of the newer Narrative Lectionary that allows preachers to stay with a whole book for longer than a week, and to develop sermon series?

2. Speaking of sermon series, we've all seen the simplistic graphics that look like self-help spam, ten steps to this or that, or glitzy movie poster themes. But if we release ourselves from the lectionary jump around, might we come up with sermon series based on, of all things, the actual Bible? Might hearing sermons on one chapter of a Gospel after another, in order, week after week after week, be the preacher's last best chance to increase the biblical literacy we miss?

IT'S ABOUT JESUS

> The goal of ministry is transformation of the world.
>
> Pastors help people live better lives.
>
> Preaching reworks Jesus Christ to make him interesting to the modern world.

Paul writes to Timothy, not on his own: *From Paul, an apostle of Christ Jesus by God's will, to promote the promise of life that is in Christ Jesus* (2 Timothy 1:1). The chief rationale for Paul's letter (or his life): *Jesus Christ.* The purpose of your life as a Christian leader: *to promote the promise of life that is in Christ Jesus*

Paul admitted to the Corinthians that he "used to know Christ by human standards" but, "that isn't how we know him now" (2 Corinthians 5:16). About Jesus, Paul's mind changed.

Me too. I thought Jesus, if we could perfect the hermeneutical tools to resurrect him, offered a new perspective on God, a better way that, if lived, would lead to an improved world, Jesus as the means to achieve a goal other than Jesus. That's not how I know him now.

I now think that Jesus is the one good reason to be in ministry, the only means of continuing over the long haul. *I thank Christ Jesus our Lord, who has given me strength because he considered me faithful. So he appointed me to ministry* (1 Timothy 1:12).

Up front, Paul is clear that Jesus is the author of his life story: *From Paul, who is an apostle of Jesus Christ by the command of God our savior and of Christ Jesus our hope* (1 Timothy 1:1).

Don't worry that, over time, Christ will become commonplace. A resurrected Christ loves to surprise. An inexhaustible resource for renewal, he refuses to have his sharp edges dulled by even the dullest of us. Rarely does Jesus's prose lapse into common sense. The constant hyperbole and intemperance found throughout First and Second Timothy are entirely due to him. An Alabama congregation wrote to complain that as bishop, I had once again sent them the wrong pastor. "Yesterday, he had the nerve to pray for the soul of Osama bin Ladin! We don't want a preacher like that."

I called the pastor, questioning his discretion. He agreed that his prayer had not been well received but, "Bishop, I was talkin' to the Lord, not them."

Well, er, yes.

"Just to put things in perspective," he continued, "I really believe that the One who commanded, 'Pray for your enemies,' just happened to be the Son of God."

There is one God and one mediator between God and humanity, the human Christ Jesus, who gave himself as a payment to set all people free. This was a testimony that was given at the right time. I was appointed to be a preacher (1 Timothy 2:5-7).

Although Paul doesn't do parables, I'm sure that I so love Jesus's parables, not only because I'm a natural born Southern storyteller but also because parables, cousins of jokes, trade in unexpected endings, so typical of the one who surprised us on Easter.

Two people go up to the Temple to pray, one a good, religious-but-not-showy, tithing Methodist like me praying, "God, I thank thee that I'm not like them." The other a disreputable creep, stands far off, beats his chest, and cries for mercy. Then the bombshell: Two go back home after service, one justified, made right with God, the other not (Luke 18:9-14).

A father had two sons, the older was dependable, hard-working, and reliable, the sort of geek esteemed by the Duke Office of Undergraduate Admissions. The younger said impudently, "Dad, drop dead. Put the will into effect. I'm outta' this hick town." The father did just that, gave him the whole inheritance. The son blew his father's hard-earned legacy on, to put it politely, "extravagant living" (Luke 15:13). When he finally came to himself and slithered home hungry and in rags the father said, "Kid, you wanted a party? I'll show you a party" (Luke 15:11-32).

The gospel's content is surprising Jesus, God reaching toward us, as one of us, *and* calling us to partner in God's grand reclamation of all creation. Thus, the story of Jesus culminates in the biggest shock of all, a resurrection hoopla with the whole of humanity, shouting, singing, prancing before the throne of the bloody Lamb. A loud voice cries, "Look! God's dwelling is here with humankind. He will dwell with them, and they will be his peoples. God himself will be with them as their God. He will wipe away every tear from their eyes. Death will be no more" (Revelation 21:3-4). At last, God's got what God wanted from the first: God with us, death slinking away in defeat. Welcome to the unending party.

God's great surprise—past, present, and future—has a human face and name, Jesus the Christ.

God Is Jesus

It wasn't just that Jesus is God. The shock is that God is Jesus. Jesus Christ is Lord; the Lord is Jesus. From the first, Jesus failed to meet expectations for how God ought to save. So down through the ages we have contrived various means of protection from God as *Christ Jesus our hope* by devising idols less surprising.

"You're Muslim [Jewish, Hindu, really into macrobiotics, avoid red meat, or whatever works for you] and I'm Christian, but we all believe in God, right?" There was a day when I thought it my duty to mouth that, doing my bit to make the world less violent because, as we all know, religious conflict is the worst and differences among believers are the bloodiest, the cause of all war and heartache. Right?

As campus minister, in almost daily contact with folks who hear "God" differently than I, combined with increased experience of Jesus, the God who is rather than the one we thought we wanted, my mind changed. Now, when somebody says innocuously, "In God we trust," or "God helps those who help themselves," or "God is unconditional love," I say obnoxiously, "Whatever God you're talking about doesn't sound like a Jew from Nazareth who lived briefly, died violently, and rose unexpectedly. I hope you won't let that end our conversation."

I thank Christ Jesus our Lord, who . . . appointed me to ministry even though I used to speak against him, attack his people, and I was proud (1 Timothy 1:12-13).

Jesus is the peculiar truth about God. As my late friend Robert Jenson put it, "God is whoever raised Jesus from the dead, having before raised Israel from Egypt."[1] (Hauerwas says that's the best theological sentence ever written.)

Christ, the one truth you know that the world doesn't without your help. Whenever the world asks, "The point of life?" or "Got hope?" or "Have something to say at my funeral?" or even, "What's your politics?" the church gives a peculiar answer: *Christ Jesus our Lord.*

"No one has ever seen God," says John's Gospel, then boasts that now we have: "God the only Son, / who is at the Father's side, / has made God known" (John 1:18). *Christ Jesus our Lord* is as much of God as we ever hope to see in this world. God up close and personal, God self-defining, God condescending, turning to us, giving us all we need to know about who God is and what God is up to.

Ask people, "What is the gospel?" many reply, "Jesus died for my sins so that when I die my soul can go to heaven." Jesus, the passive automaton who was briefly among us and trudged to his death to pay for our ticket to eternity.

153

Too much is left out. Jesus's life detached from his death, and Christ's salvation becomes a quiz that, if passed, leads to your optimum individual eternal destination. Your relationship with God reduced to a transaction that's dependent upon your astute believing, wise deciding, deep feeling, or good behaving. This, good news?

Ask around campus, "What is the gospel?" I bet you'll hear, "Jesus reveals God's way to us. He loved everyone, especially children and people with disabilities, and judged nobody. We ought to live that way too, working for peace with justice for the transformation of the world." Our relationship with God is contingent on us. This, good news?

Good News: Jesus demonstrates that our friendship with God is God's self-assigned task. Jesus wants more than a "personal relationship" and is unsatisfied just pointing the way. He is the way, truth, and life, Lord who wants nothing less than to be light for the whole darkened world. But he will accomplish enlightenment in his peculiar way, resisting our attempts to force him to be the savior he is not.

Love in Action

The New Testament, enlivened by the fully human/fully revealing, present Christ, is the most reliable source for thinking about Jesus. On a near weekly basis Scripture refuses to be compliant or to smooth down Jesus, though that's never kept us from trying to make him more manageable.

As I've said, vague, sentimental "love" is the Jesus substitute of the moment in my neighborhood. "God is love," the gospel condensed to a bumper sticker. Who needs Jesus to tell us that we ought to love one another?

"It's all about love," goes down easier than "It's all about Jesus," because blurring the gospel into an impersonal generality like "love" implies that the problem between us and God can be solved by us. All we need is love, which we are then free to define as we please. You're loving, lovely, and loveable, in your better moments, so, as a preacher, urge everyone else to be that way too. Come on, be the best that you can be. Love one another.

Who would kill somebody for saying that?

(Barbara Brown Taylor began a Lenten sermon in Duke Chapel, "Ever had somebody tell you something about yourself that was so painfully true that you wanted to murder them? Well, now you know why we crucified Jesus.")

Paul's famous hymn to love, 1 Corinthians 13—extolling love as greater even than faith and hope—is a darling at weddings. (Strange. As you know, Paul wasn't a fan of matrimony.) It's actually a hymn sung by a divided congregation about the only way to get along with each other in church: a dogged determination to love and be loved among the unlovable and the unlovely in the same way Christ has loved us.

Maybe that's why John's Jesus doesn't tell his disciples "love your neighbor" (Mark 12:31) but rather "love each other" (John 13:34). Make love with fellow believers in church. Anybody who thinks that John's Gospel thereby makes love easier by making it in house, churchy, and parochial isn't in the current mudslinging UMC divorce nor has served on a congregation's Finance Committee. Maybe that's why Jesus commanded, rather than suggested, love among the baptized (John 13:34).

The gospel reduced to "love your neighbor" doesn't explain why Jesus prepared for his ministry, not with seminary in New Haven, but with forty days of famine in the wilderness. There, Satan confronted him (Luke 4:1-13).

(Don't you find interesting that Jesus's most extended conversation with Satan occurred in his first days of ministry, suggesting that it's early, as you are learning the habits and forming the tone and patterns of your ministry, that Satan is most likely present? But that's another sermon.)

"Since you are God's Son," mocks Satan, "command this stone to become a loaf of bread" (Luke 4:3). Cure world hunger! Jesus refused.

True, give hungry people bread today, they'll be hungry tomorrow. How about political power to do lasting good by controlling all the nations? "Worship me!" (Luke 4:7). Jesus refused. (Here, I'll resist the temptation to belabor that Satan bragged of owning all the nations. Did, at some point, the Lord say, "Politics? Not my thing. Here, Satan, the U.N. is yours"?)

After these rebuffs, as last resort, Satan goes spiritual. Miraculously overcome all suffering and death. Fear of death, Phobia Number One. Right?

Jesus refused. Feeding the hungry, ending war, defeat of death, are not these worthy goods?

Satan slinks away until a "more opportune time" (Luke 4:13).

Whatever Jesus's mission, it's not accomplished by a display of power and glory nor by force, using Satan's mechanisms.

Later, as Jesus hung from his cross, Satan at last found his "more opportune time." The democratic mob mocks Jesus, "Since you are the Son of God, act like it. Throw yourself down from that cross. Let's see your power and glory." At Golgotha, Satan's words are now on our lips (Matthew 27:40). Jesus just hangs there, stretching out his wounded, bloody arms as if in embrace, blessing his executioners, thereby forever redefining, "God is love."

The Politics of Jesus

Out of seminary, back in South Carolina Methodism, I scoffed at benighted laity who urged, "Stick to saving souls and stay out of politics." I was the left-wing, long-haired firebrand preaching, "Come on people, we can save the world! Vote a straight Democratic ticket."

My mind changed. I discovered that Jesus's quarrel with the world was fiercer than politics of the left or the right. The kingdom of heaven required more than electing a few enlightened senators, Jesus's resurrection having rendered secular, democratic (*that is,* godless) politics obsolete.

Here's Jesus's platform, unveiled at his first sermon:

The Spirit of the Lord is upon me,
> because the Lord has anointed me.
He has sent me to preach good news to the poor,
> to proclaim release to the prisoners
> and recovery of sight to the blind,
> to liberate the oppressed,
> and to proclaim the year of the Lord's favor. (Luke 4:18-19)

Jesus then preaches, contemporizing Isaiah's ancient words. "Today, this scripture has been fulfilled just as you heard it" (Luke 4:21). Excitement stirs through the congregation. At last God has come for us because, after all, who is more deserving of release and liberation than God's own family who suffer the empire's injustice?

Note that the folk at Nazareth loved how Jesus read Scripture. "Hard to believe that's Mary and Joe's boy. He reads so well, doesn't he?" Then Jesus begins to preach and (preacher take note!) that's where the trouble starts:

"Let's see, the last acceptable year God came among us, during the days of the prophet Elijah, there had to be many hungry widows in Israel. God's prophet fed only a non-Jewish, pagan woman. There must have been many sick Israelites but Elisha healed only Naaman, a Syrian army officer," or words to that effect (Luke 4:25-27).

The congregation didn't like being reminded (from their own Scripture!) that God's love had worked the other side of the street before and might do so again. Hear, O Israel, there is one God whose love isn't limited to us and those whom we love (Deuteronomy 6:4). God's love is like Jesus who embodies the peculiar politics that he announces.

The congregation responds in unison, "Let's kill him."

On their way to toss the preacher over a cliff, surely one exclaimed, "Never seen this congregation more united!"

Mother Mary had forewarned with her war chant of a lullaby:

He shows mercy to everyone, . . .
> He has shown strength with his arm.
He has scattered those with arrogant thoughts and proud
inclinations.
> He has pulled the powerful down from their thrones
> > and lifted up the lowly.
He has filled the hungry with good things
> and sent the rich away empty-handed.
He has come to the aid of his servant Israel,
> > remembering his mercy,
> just as he promised to our ancestors,
> > to Abraham and to Abraham's descendants forever.
(Luke 1:50-55)

Welcome to the revolution.

Jesus wasn't crucified for, "Love your neighbor." His redefinition of love, in his person and in his preaching, was an embodied, political revolt against worldly regimes based on the fear of death (and aren't they all?). Death is done by every government, democratic or not. We now believe that it's crazy to die for God but noble to sacrifice our children for the U.S.A., the government, sole lord over life and death. Thus, we pour millions into health care, "homeland security," erect border walls, and take the lives of criminals out of love for our families. Death denial, death avoidance, and death dread explain so much.

For all of his contributions and achievements, John Wesley's bust sits cold upon my shelf, and I'm not feeling all that well myself. Paul preaches politics by reminding Timothy that nobody decisively deals with death but Christ. He *alone has immortality. . . . Honor and eternal power belong to him. . . . I command you in the presence of God, who gives life to all things, and Christ Jesus, who made the good confession when testifying before Pontius Pilate* (1 Timothy 6:16, 13).

Why, in talking about Jesus, would Paul bring up political hack and murderer, Pilate (1 Timothy 6:13)? You will recall that on his way to be tortured to death, Jesus was interrogated by Pilate, Roman lord over life and death: "So they tell me that you are the King of Jews? Can that be true?"

Jesus replied, "My kingdom isn't from here" (John 18:36).

Jesus's kingdom isn't just a reiteration of Rome. He doesn't deny kingship. "You say that I am a king. I was born and came into the world for this reason: to testify to the truth. Whoever accepts the truth listens to my voice" (John 18:37).

Pilate responds with a philosophical shrug, "What is truth?" (John 18:38).

The truth is that Jesus, King of truth, has come to establish a new polis that tells the truth, a true family, a beachhead of resident aliens who are God's alternative politics based not, as other governments, on our collective fear of death, but on the truth of his resurrection. I'm talking about your congregation.

What is truth? "I am the truth," says Jesus (John 14:6). The world's truth is kill or be killed, the way to peace is war, where there's breath, that's life, where there's death, there's no hope, life is a right to be protected and defended to the death. We have, within our power, to be immortal, given the right funding for medical research. Money? At the end, the one with the most toys wins. Stranger? Build a wall. Crime? Punishment. Threat? Get yourself a gun. Beloved, deadly, political lies.

Jesus is not "from here." He is truth personified, embodied in the one who lived briefly, died violently, rose unexpectedly, *and* assembled a crowd of preachers like us and our people to tell the whole world about it whether Pilate wants to hear it or not. If this be not true, we'd better pack up, get on the bus, and go home.

Making Jesus Attractive

Alas, a chief sin of us preachers is to attempt to sidestep the politics of Jesus by stressing the personal blessings that he offers rather than the politically charged, demanding truth he is. Lonely? Come to church and you'll make friends. Anxious? The Prince of Peace will fix that. Traumatized? Jesus heals. Guilty? Christ forgives. Having a tough time right now? Try Jesus, you'll feel better in the morning.

Bread, immortality, and power, Satan's tempting offers now on the lips of us preachers.

Yes, Jesus occasionally heals, feeds the hungry, and stills troubled waters. And yet, these sporadic, miraculous blessings are not the good news. Maybe that's why, sometimes when he healed someone, he commanded them to keep it to themselves (Matthew 9:30; Mark 1:43-44). Never did Jesus say, call me "The Great Physician."

The gospel is the announcement of a new regime that's inaugurated solely by the life, death, and resurrection of Christ. Real-world, real-time embodiment of truth, God's love in action, the politics of Jesus, your congregation.

To suffer having our lives taken, rather than to take life, to know that this life, good as it is, is not all there is and worse can happen to us than death, that the world has not within its worldly means to make peace, that life is not a right, it's a gift, that any hope for life beyond this life is that the story of the death and resurrection of Jesus is true. Wisdom, Jesus's style.

Want life? Die. Money? Give it away. Stranger? Show hospitality and welcome. Crime? Forgiveness, reparation, restoration. Threat? Lean on the Lord. Enemies? Well, we all know what he commanded us to do with those who hate us.

We try to weasel out of Jesus's platform. "Well, Jesus was the Son of God so practice of his peculiar politics was easy for him." Then along comes Chalcedon, insisting that Jesus wasn't nearly human; he was fully, one hundred percent human. His way can't be dismissed as an impossible, divine ideal.

In the same breath Chalcedon says that he was one hundred percent God so we can't shelve his gospel saying, "It's hard to know whose side God is on," or, "Who knows what God wants from us?" or, "Can't say for sure what God's up to."

In the church basement, at the Wednesday morning men's breakfast (Jesus and a sausage biscuit at an ungodly hour) gun control was up for debate. Half the group said that there are too many guns, making defense of one's family difficult. Get guns off the streets. The others said that we live in a violent society where the bad guys have guns so we good guys must protect ourselves with more guns.

I chortled, "Well, at least we all agree, 'Defense of our families is the main point,' though we differ on the means."

One man (an accountant!) asked, "Preacher, is there any instance of self-defense in the New Testament?" Oops. If you can't be for self-defense, what can you be for?

You can be for the one who said, "I'm the way, the truth, and the life," God's answer to a culture of death.

As preacher, you're sure to have moments when you are made freshly aware that one blessing Jesus never promised was safety. Repeatedly he predicted, even promised, suffering along with freedom from the natural, expected human anxiety that afflicts us, liberation from our self-inflicted, self-destructive fears.

The cross is not a bad back or a difficult-to-get-along-with relative. "Cross" is the predictable suffering, rejection, and maybe even death that could come your way because you are walking Jesus's way, a path counter to the world's way. He said to take up the cross daily (Luke 9:23). (I'm doing well to go cruciform once a month, much less daily.) Our questions tend not to be, "Why did Jesus suffer for us?" but "Why must we suffer because of Jesus? Why does Jesus allow people to beat up on his friends?"

Yet when we've done our worst—put to death God's Son—God takes our sin and puts Jesus in charge of our salvation. Remember that next time you either do or receive the worst.

When you are going through a time of pain that's inflicted by your church (and you will), family, marriage, friends, or enemies (No enemies? Check the substance of your sermons.), you are justified in considering that your pain could be validation of your fidelity to the way, truth, and life, proof that your preaching is not as cowardly and compromised as you may have feared.

What else could Paul have been thinking when he claimed, "We even take pride in our problems" (Romans 5:3)?

Christ Present

Paul seldom shows interest in the details of Jesus's earthly life and ministry. Jesus's parables and sermons, which have been so helpful to my preaching, are not for Paul. Little of the Gospels' accounts of Jesus make it into Paul's letters, especially his letters to Timothy, even though Paul's letters predate the Gospels.

Why? Paul is laser focused upon the resurrected, active presence of Jesus. No mere historical personage to be reconstructed from past memory, Jesus is here, now. Nor does Paul attempt systematic presentation of the substance of the teachings of Jesus. What we've got is Jesus, here, now, "I have been crucified with Christ and I no longer live, but Christ lives in me" (Galatians 2:20).

Jesus Christ, who was raised from the dead and descended from David. This is my good news. This is the reason I'm suffering to the point that I'm in prison like a common criminal. But God's word cannot be imprisoned (2 Timothy 2:8-9). Paul's good news is not teaching about Jesus or teaching from Jesus, it's Jesus Christ, who was raised from the dead. Paul never got over the wonder, the surprise, the scandal that to one "born at the wrong time" (1 Corinthians 15:7-8), Christ not only appeared but also called and stuck with him.

Paul tells the Corinthians that he "passed on to you as most important what I also received: Christ died for our sins in line with the scriptures, he was buried, and he rose on the third day in line with the scriptures," the barest summary of the major historical claims of the faith (1 Corinthians 15:3-4). As astounding as what Jesus did back then, the risen Christ "appeared to Cephas, then to the Twelve, and then he appeared to more than five hundred brothers and sisters at once—most of them are still alive to this day, though some have died. Then he appeared to James, then to all the apostles, and last of all he appeared to me, as if I were born at the wrong time" (1 Corinthians 15:5-8).

What impresses Paul was not that a corpse was resuscitated but that Christ kept showing up, even to those "born at the wrong time." Which, when you think about it, is all of us belatedly born to whom Christ has appeared.

In his resurrection Jesus defeated death and came back to us promising, "Look, I myself will be with you every day until the end of this present age" (Matthew 28:20). Easter ends not only the rule of Death but also our fear of Godforsakeness. If you don't believe that's true, or are not actively on your way to believing that, ministry is misery.

Now his grace is revealed through the appearance of our savior, Christ Jesus. He destroyed death and brought life and immortality into clear focus through the good news. I was appointed a messenger, apostle, and teacher of this good news (2 Timothy 1:10-11).

Better than resuscitation of a dead body, resurrection is vindication of crucified Jesus. Much more than return of the robin in the spring, a butterfly emerging from the cocoon, or Jesus living on in the disciples' memories, resurrection is God's decisive, eternal "No!" to the forces of sin and death that nailed Jesus to the cross. The one who forgave his crucifiers, who reached out to sinner and outcast, who stood up to the authorities and spoke of a world shifting on its axis through suffering love, the one who invited everybody to jump on board his revolution and was brutally nailed to a cross for it, he's the only one God ever raised from the dead.

Easter is God's victory, God's grand self-attestation as if to say, "You want to know who I am, where I'm headed, look to the only one raised from the dead." Once you lay aside your prejudices and dare to believe the women running from the tomb, so much about Jesus falls into place. On the other hand, if Jesus has not been resurrected, little that the church (or Paul) claims about Christ makes sense.

Said the district superintendent to the pleading pastor, "Okay, you say you can't move to that part of Alabama because it's as bad as Mississippi and, as you put it, 'that church is dead, died ten years ago, and it would kill me to be sent to a dead church.'"

"I'll tell the bishop you don't want to go but, let me warn you, this bishop literally believes in the bodily resurrection of Jesus Christ. So to say, 'That church is dead,' don't mean nothin' to him. Bishop thinks he's givin' you an opportunity to confirm his theology of Easter."

I'm unworthy of such accusation

No resurrected Christ, no hope. They're resurrection Christ appearances, not resuscitation sightings. Christ's contemporary presence is pure gift. In his resurrection appearances we learned it ain't over between us and God until God says it's over, that our sin doesn't stump a God determined to be our God. Because of resurrection, Christians don't do dejection and we pastors are forbidden to say, "People don't change," or, "It's hopeless, nothing to be done."

Remember Jesus Christ, who was raised from the dead and descended from David. This is my good news. This is the reason I'm suffering to the point that I'm in prison like a common criminal. But God's word cannot be imprisoned. This is why I endure everything for the sake of those who are chosen by God so that they too may experience salvation in Christ Jesus with eternal glory (2 Timothy 2:8-10).

Resurrected Jesus is not just love; he's love in action, love refusing defeat by death, love alive and busy, loving the unlovable and unlovely even without our asking to be loved. Our labors are not the sole effort, and death never gets the last word. A resurrected God insists on bringing something fresh into every situation, even the worst. The God of exodus and homecoming after Israel's exile loves to surprise. Though Jesus's ministry in Judea was impressive, what he may do in your town right now, using you, even you, is as remarkable.

Michelangelo Caravaggio, *The Calling of St. Matthew,*
San Luigi dei Francesi, Rome, 1599–1600

See Christ barge into Matthew's den of publican thieves like he owns the place, thrusting his hand toward the wrong person, "Follow me." The only source of light in the darkened room is Jesus. His outthrust hand is a quote from Caravaggio's mentor, Michelangelo. Sistine Chapel "Creation." Get it? Whenever Jesus appears, uninvited, and puts the finger on you, wrong though you are, the Stranger on the Shore reaching toward you, that's the beginning of a whole new world, Christ not waiting for final resurrection to shake things up, Christ calling the unlikeliest of sinners to join his Easter commotion.

The first thing done by the risen Christ? He goes looking for his dim-witted disciples, returning to the same Galilean knuckleheads who betrayed and disappointed him. One would think that on the first day of your resurrected life you would burst into the palace in Jerusalem saying, "Pilate. You made a big mistake. It's payback time."

No, the risen Christ returns to outback Galilee. They didn't go looking for him; once again, he turns to them and then turns them out into the whole world, probably saying, "One more time. Catch people!"

"I myself will be with you every day until the end of this present age," he promises (Matthew 28:20), as if to say, "I had but a few years to harass you before I was murdered by people who, seen from my cross, looked a lot like you. After resurrection, I am with you always. You'll never get God off your back." The Easter mandate? "Go! Fish! Tell somebody! He's back, for good!" (see Matthew 28:10).

Body Building

Jesus advocated no program of human reform, recommended no collective social adjustments, no matter how badly needed or enlightened, never wrote a book or squirrelled away a pension (ouch!). Jesus was not into ethical codes, had no ideology, did no interesting work in political science and social ethics, and never put forth a plan of action, other than the seemingly wildly impractical notions that the first will be last, that we must turn the other cheek to those who strike us, forgive our enemies, find our lives by losing them, and become like clueless, ignorant, dependent little children.

What Jesus did was save us by adopting us into his family, the church, making salvation a group thing. Not waiting for people wanting to be saved, he sought them out for salvage, putting them in an entourage (church) whether or not they liked their traveling companions.

For all its faults, Paul says that Timothy's church *is the church of the living God and the backbone and support of the truth* (1 Timothy 3:15). This church?

"For where two or three are gathered in my name," he promised, "I'm there with them" (Matthew 18:20). It's hard to think of someone as "present" who is not bodily present. Even in his resurrection, Christ had a body. When some of his disciples failed to recognize him in his resurrected body, he showed them the holes in his hands, the wound in his side, and ate some leftover fish. Seeing is believing. Bodily proof, irrefutable. That's Jesus. He remembers that we have bodies and our bodies have us. So he gives us tangible, visible, sacramental evidence in order to believe. We come to church, a piece of bread is put in our hands with the words, "The *body* of Christ, given for you." Paul's favorite designation of the church? Christ's body (1 Corinthians 12:27).

As someone who writes books, I'm embarrassed that Jesus never had the need to publish anything, leaving no constitution, set of ethical guidelines, collection of noble sayings, nor founding document. His body is his primary way of revealing himself to the world and bringing the world to himself. Christ's body, the church, the way Christ takes up room, his visible, corporeal presence, his gift, physical proof of his reign.

After all his scathing criticisms of Timothy's church, Paul astounds by saying that the church, this church, warts and all, *is the church of the living God and the backbone and support of the truth* (1 Timothy 3:15). Us? The church, yes, even the diminished UMC, Inc., is Christ's visible, bodily appeal to the world. Jesus could have established an efficient system of public welfare or founded an ethical improvement colloquium. Instead, gathering ordinary people with a reckless, "Follow me!" he invited us to be his revolution.

Because Americans are in a decidedly anti-institutional mood, "spirituality" is all the rage—feeling religious, sort of—church without the bother of people who fail to be as vaguely, innocuously spiritual as you. "Spirituality"—Jesus on the cheap, without a bride or a body, a king without a kingdom, Jesus stripped of sinners like you and me.

Everybody would love Jesus if he were spiritual. Believing that your congregation, with its flaws and failings, is *the backbone and support of the truth,* nothing less than the body of Christ, requires a leap of faith.

It's a heck of a way for Christ to show himself to the world. Still, it's his way of refusing dismissal as an apolitical, disincarnate, spiritual blur.

As a pastor/preacher you've been set aside by the church for convening, enlarging, protecting, and keeping the church, church. Your significance has been hitched to the ragtag, full of holes, wounded crowd assembled at your church.

"As a prisoner for the Lord, I encourage you to live as people worthy of the call you received from God. . . . Accept each other with love, and make an effort to preserve the unity of the Spirit with the peace that ties you together. You are one body and one spirit, just as God also called you in one hope. There is one Lord, one faith, one baptism, and one God and Father of all, who is over all, through all, and in all" (Ephesians 4:1-6).

How does Christ accomplish "unity" and "peace" in the church? "He gave some apostles, some prophets, some evangelists, and some pastors and teachers. His purpose was to equip God's people for the work of serving and building up the body of Christ until we all reach the unity of faith and knowledge of God's Son" (Ephesians 4:11-13). You, Christ's gift to his church to "equip God's people for the work."

Though the point of your life is to worry about and to nurture the church, am I right in assuming that the most difficult aspect of your work is the church?

The church is a mess; but it always has been. When lamenting the disunity in your congregation, take comfort that Paul wouldn't so frequently harp on the need for unity, peace, and love if his congregants were not divided, fighting, and disdainful of one another.

Nobody withdraws from a congregation saying, "Jesus asks too much." You think they would, considering the demands and commands of Christ. They leave muttering, "Love Jesus; can't stand his friends."

In my efforts as evangelist, never had anyone reject the gospel because of something Jesus said or did, though he makes some outrageous demands. It's the church, to whom has been given the command to make disciples, his present, crucified body, that's the greatest impediment to attracting more disciples. As dear Flannery put it, "You have to suffer as much from the Church as for it."[2]

Still, church is where Christ insists that we name these oddballs "brother," "sister," and that we allow ourselves to be called the same by them. Church gives us something good to do with gifts we've been given. Christian believing is a group product, not a discovery of the solitary individual. In church we learn dependency upon others (some of them dead for a thousand years) who help us endure the rigors of discipleship. Church is life together with Jesus here, now, yes, even with the chair of your church's trustees with his Neanderthal political opinions, halitosis, and exaggerated opinion of himself topped off with a negative view of you. What Jesus sees in him, maybe one day you will know.

Jesus Speaks for Himself

I'm happy to report that in spite of insults and wounds we have inflicted upon his body, the church, notwithstanding all the ways we've attempted to house-train this born troublemaker, resurrected Jesus is quite able to rise up, assert himself, and claim his people. If he didn't, left to our own devices we'd make ministry trivial, inconsequential, and therefore humanly convenient.

Weaseling myself into the undergrad curriculum, I proposed a class, "Jesus: Most Interesting Person in the World." When the Curriculum Committee refused approval, saying they feared the class would be perceived as a means of proselyting, I shot back, "You obviously know nothing of Methodists. It's been so long since we've converted anybody, we've forgotten how. The students' atheism is safe with me."

I cunningly changed the title to, "Jesus Through the Centuries," and snuck it through as a history course on how people viewed Jesus in different historical epochs.

First class I whispered to the students, "Jesus is of interest, not as an historical figure but because some of us think he's present, here, now. You want history, go study George Washington. You can pin him down and dissect him like a cadaver. He's dead. Jesus isn't."

During the semester we examined the many Searches for the Historical Jesus, read Strauss, Schweitzer, Borg, and others who attempted to put a leash on Jesus.

The last class I sighed, "I'm now wondering if this class was a mistake."

"You've waited until the end to tell us that?" a student snorted.

"I mean, here we sit in the middle of this placid campus," I explained. "I say something civil, then you cordially say something back, we think about it, then we all go out and lie on the grass and look up at the trees. Problem is, our subject is Jesus, wild troublemaker, criminalized and incarcerated by a consortium of government and religious officials who tortured him to death. I fear we've done an injustice to the subject of our inquiry.

"Like, if you have never been honest to God hungry, if you are happy with the status quo and are tight with the administration, if you have never been treated like a criminal and done jail time," I pled, "I'm not a good enough professor to explicate Jesus to you."

"I have," said the long-haired, sullen student who had spent most classes smirking, arms folded in contempt.

"Have what?" I asked.

"Done jail time. Three nights that I'll never get over as long as I live. I don't fear hell 'cause I've been there, done that."

With tears I said, "Son, though I have spent my life working for Jesus, and can read the original Greek, you may be closer to Jesus than I.

"Right now, I'm hearing Jesus snicker, 'The wrong guy taught this class.'"

Questions from United Methodist pastor, Jason Micheli, author of *A Quid Without Any Quo: Gospel Freedom According to Galatians* and host of Crackers and Grape Juice podcast:

1. One of your gifts to the church and preachers is the winsome way you present discipleship as adventure. By going on an adventure with Jesus and being given a life bigger than otherwise, you eliminate the homiletical distinction between exhortation and proclamation. Nearer the end of your ministry than its beginning, what counsel have you for pastors who no longer feel the sense of adventure that occasioned their call?

2. Twenty-four years into my ministry, I've realized that seminary did me a disservice by present-ing the church fathers and creedal councils as Church History. In what ways do you think the ancient church can make the modern world more interesting to Jesus? And what role do you see for the sacraments—a topic that figures less in your preaching—in ministry in a post-Christian culture?

3. I, too, entered ministry thinking it was my role to be helpful and loving rather than truthful. Despite your reputation, I know you to be an effective pastoral presence. How do you think we can best apply the gospel in pastoral situations—absolving sin, offering a promise, etc.?

GOD BE WITH YOU

> Human need is so great, the world's ills so many, and the church so lethargic. As pastor it's up to me to work conscientiously to set things right.
>
> Fortunately, God has blessed me with gifts; it's my duty busily to utilize those gifts no matter what.

The Lord be with your spirit. Grace be with you all (2 Timothy 4:22).

For Compline, the *Book of Common Prayer* has a perfect prayer for the completion of a pastor's busy day:

Keep watch, dear Lord, with those who work, or watch, or weep this night, and give your angels charge over those who sleep. Tend the sick, Lord Christ; give rest to the weary, bless the dying, soothe the suffering, pity the afflicted, shield the joyous; and all for your love's sake. Amen.

You're thinking, "It takes chutzpa for you, a priest, as you turn out the lights and call it a day, to tell the Lord to watch, give, tend, bless, soothe, and pity. Isn't that your job?"

I say it takes realism to admit that most of what we and our people need, at the end of the day, is not ours to give.

"Lord, I'm clocking out. The rest is up to you," I pray as I leave next Sunday's sermon unfinished, Clara James unvisited, George still drinking, Tom and Joe unreconciled, the budget broke, and much of the world still in the dark about who God is and what God's up to.

In similar fashion, Paul ends with benediction, *May grace be with you all* (1 Timothy 6:21).

Paul pronounces benediction upon Timothy and his churches because it's up to God to accomplish good through their ministry or good won't be done. Earlier, I railed at the modern world's robbery of God's agency, rendering the Trinity into a deity who is allegedly compassionate, but never gets around to actually doing anything, supposedly caring, but hands off, uninvolved.

As shadows lengthen, at the end, when all has been said and done, there's so much left undone that we must believe in God's active agency watching, giving, tending, blessing, soothing, and pitying or ministry is doomed to despair.

I'm thankful that my flaccid theology has been enriched, enlarged, and enlivened by God's assigning me the humanly impossible task of preaching the gospel. Despondency over ministry's unfeasibility drove me into the arms of a merciful God, forcing me to change my mind: God is love in action, providentially engaged, busy among us, getting back what belongs to God.

The Lord be with your spirit. Grace be with you all (2 Timothy 4:22).

Years ago I did research for a book about the then current craze of "clergy burnout." I learned that a major factor in clergy calling it quits was that the work is never finished. "How I envy housepainters," one ex-pastor told me. "At the end of the day they get to step back and say, 'Look what I did.'"

An early review of my *Pastor: The Theology and Practice of Ordained Ministry* howled, "If a pastor takes this book to heart, and attempts to do all that Willimon claims is absolutely necessary, he'll drop dead of exhaustion." Did I overstate the need for, and the value of, competence and hard work in the pastoral ministry?

Blame it on my Methodism. One of John Wesley's favorite texts (sending Lutherans through the roof) was, Paul's "Work out your own salvation with fear and trembling" (Philippians 2:12 KJV). I mean *work*. Nobody outpaced the do-gooding of early Methodists. Sadly, when later day Methodists lost a strong sense of God's agency, presence, and providence, our originating Arminianism morphed into full on Pelagianism. Mother, I'd rather do it myself. Take a deep breath, try hard, we can set things right between us and God, if we put our shoulder to the wheel. Why limit ourselves to sanctifying South Carolina. Come on, gang, let's transform the world!

The less committed among us excused ourselves with, "I'm only human," or, "Things didn't go as planned. I'm peddling as fast as I can." The more conscientious breathlessly attempted to save ourselves, to set right the world by ourselves, as if Jesus had retired and the Holy Spirit had moved on, leaving us to ourselves. Little wonder pastoral lassitude is epidemic.

Who would blame Timothy for exhausting himself as a frenetic, works-righteousness, spiritual busy-beaver do-gooder if he took seriously Paul's repeated to-do lists?

But as for you, man of God, run away from all these things. Instead, pursue righteousness, holy living, faithfulness, love, endurance, and gentleness. Compete in the good fight of faith. Grab hold of eternal life. . . . I command you in the presence of God, . . . Obey this order without fault or failure until the appearance of our Lord Jesus Christ (1 Timothy 6:11-14).

Paul, more Methodist than Lutheran.

"An overworked pastor is an incompetent," asserted a veteran church coach.

I countered, "An overloaded pastor is probably a parson with an inadequate theology of providence."

Which may be why Paul begins talking to Timothy, not with a list of things he just must do to succeed in ministry but with blessing, as if to remind Timothy up-front that this is a three-way. Before Paul tells Timothy to do anything for God, Paul blesses him with providential grace, mercy, and peace from God:

From Paul, an apostle of Christ Jesus by God's will, to promote the promise of life that is in Christ Jesus.

To Timothy, my dear child.

Grace, mercy, and peace from God the Father and Christ Jesus our Lord (2 Timothy 1:1-2).

Nothing that Paul urges is to be undertaken bereft of God's blessing.

That's why I've long thought that blessing, the benediction at the end of a service, is for us pastor/preachers, the highlight of worship, and the most theologically significant of pastoral acts.

Blessed to Bless

Timothy need not be intimidated by the outrageously long lists of duties Paul assigns in these letters. Neither Paul nor Timothy work alone. At best, church leaders do advance preparation for, or mopping up after, God's commandeering of our people. God is not only with us but also working for us and on us, sometimes in spite of us. Therefore, we preachers are free recklessly to throw ourselves into our work, or take the day off, knowing that God will not allow us to thwart God's intentions for the world.

The Lord be with your spirit. Grace be with you all (2 Timothy 4:22).

Blessing is the main job assigned to priests by the Lord. We are to "place my name" on the people of Israel:

The LORD spoke to Moses: Tell Aaron and his sons: You will bless the Israelites as follows. Say to them:

The LORD bless you and protect you.
The LORD make his face shine on you and be gracious to you.
The LORD lift up his face to you and grant you peace.

They will place my name on the Israelites, and I will bless them.
(Numbers 6:22-27)

Not an inappropriate job description for clergy; we lay God's name upon people then enjoy what God does with them.

The one who blesses is God, through our words and gestures, as in the benediction we lay God's name on them. In our blessing, the Lord blesses, protects, makes, lifts, and grants. A blessing isn't a prayer; it's a commendation of God's people to God. Jesus blessed children (Mark 10:13-16), meals (Mark 6:41; 8:6-7, and most notably, the last supper, Mark 14:22). Jesus blessed his disciples (Luke 24:50-51) and then ordered his disciples to go out, not only to preach but also to bless anybody along the road, even those who curse them (Luke 6:28).

Such wide, reckless expection of benediction is expected of a God who boundlessly blesses with warm sun and life-giving rain both the righteous and the unrighteous, the good, the bad, and the ugly, you and me (Matthew 5:45). Paul chimes in, "Bless people who harass you—bless and don't curse them" (Romans 12:14). Even my loathable IRD and GMC harassers? It is wise not to trust them, even with your laundry, but you do have to bless them. Luke says that Jesus's last act before his Ascension was to bless those whom he had called: "He led them out as far as Bethany, where he lifted his hands and blessed them. As he blessed them, he left them and was taken up to heaven" (Luke 24:50-51).

The Lord be with your spirit. Grace be with you all (2 Timothy 4:22).

Jesus tells his disciples to bless the poor, the hungry, and those who weep or are despised (Luke 6:20-22). Prophetic rebuke, moral correction, exhortation, healing, and orthodox theology must defer to blessing as the major business of the church; healthy churches are always looking for ways to bless their surrounding communities.

The steadfast, covenantal love of God, divine presence, spirit, and grace, even for those who curse us, all in this human gesture of blessing that is our duty, no, our joy as pastors to lay upon God's people. Huge theological claims are made every time we stand before our people, arms outstretched, look them in the eye, and say, "God be with you."

We are not abandoning them to heartless fate, leaving them to grope their way through the world, or giving them their assignments for the week. We are commending them to the God who, during this time of worship, entrusted them to us. The French *adieu*, the Spanish *adios*, the English *good-bye*, though now emptied of theological significance, have their origins in, "God be with you."

Blessing is an affirmation that God doesn't stop creating after Genesis 1. We've never been left to our own devices. Therein is our hope, in life, in death, in any life beyond death. It's not all up to us. "My Father is still working, and I am working too" (John 5:17).

Thus, Flannery O'Connor advises those who have difficulty believing to at least "keep an open mind" and "leave the rest to God."[1]

It's not up to me to bring in the kingdom of God. I can't preach a sermon that's the last word on God. In blessing, I leave the rest up to God, sending the flock forth in confidence that God will providentially continue the conversation that may have begun with my sermon but will keep intruding upon their lives in ways that I can't. So very determined is Jesus to have them as his own, we are able confidently to pronounce with Paul, *The Lord be with your spirit* (2 Timothy 4:22).

I hope you don't think it an overstatement for me to assert that the ability to bless is the test of whether someone ought to be trusted to be pastor of a congregation. The bodily gesture of blessing, done with authority and conviction, audibly, visibly in front of a congregation is a sign, indeed an enactment of the Christological reality that gathers, guides, sends us forth, and goes out with us. Blessing, done well, at the conclusion of worship, is a wonderful antidote for a North American church that's often squeamish about strong theological assertions of Providence.

Some of my most treasured moments in ministry have been when I was able to bless the kid from the church youth group who, having been convicted, was entering the Youth Correctional Center, but not without my benediction. "Just remember. Paul did time in a joint like this," I consoled him. "The Lord be with you and bless you."

Then there was the time I raised my hands in blessing of a congregation that had just learned that they were six months arears in their mortgage payments and didn't know if they would make it until next Sunday. I also was fortunate enough to bless the Jones family when they departed for a faraway town, or said grace over the poor soul who confessed to me, gesturing toward his refrigerator, "I think the bottle will kill me."

As I left comatose Janet in her hospital room, after her stroke, and the doctor pulled out the feeding tube saying, "She's on her own now," I responded, "No she isn't."

I laid hands on her head, just like some pastor before me had done at her baptism, glad that I could say to Janet, whether she heard me or not, "The Lord bless you and keep you, the Lord make his face shine on you and be gracious to you. The LORD lift up his face to you and grant you peace."

I hope you are comfortable and confident in your stewardship of this powerful gesture. My first week as bishop, a veteran church observer told me, "As bishop, you won't be doing much actual work. The main job of a bishop is to bless. You will bless clergy at ordinations, bless parsonages, say grace at dinners in church basements, and on occasion even bless a redecorated fellowship hall."

Then he leaned in close and whispered, "God help you if you bless infidelity." It was an apt warning. Jesus didn't just bless the poor; he cursed the rich (Luke 6:20-49). On one occasion Jesus even cussed a barren fig tree, though figs were out of season (Mark 11:12-25). My take on this wilted fig tree: God help us if, by tacitly blessing unfruitful disciples, slovenly discipleship, or cowardly, introverted refusal to witness, we bless infidelity.

Don't tell 'em, "This is the most loving, caring congregation," unless it's true.

Living Reminder

Henri Nouwen's *The Living Reminder* is my favorite of Henri's meditations on ministry.[2] That's us. We clergy are bodily present, in the flesh, real time, living reminders of Christ. We remind others, not in a historical sense but as, "Remember who you are." The blessed. Thus Paul urges Timothy to remind his flock that God goes with them. *Remind them of these things . . .* (2 Timothy 2:14). We can't save, but we can remind, on a weekly basis, that God does. We can't be with them, guiding, correcting, criticizing, and sustaining them as they go forth, but God can. *Remember Jesus Christ, who was raised from the dead and descended from David. This is my good news* (2 Timothy 2:8).

Remember, as you exit this service, or that difficult conversation, or even depart this life, God goes with you. You belong to Christ. Your life is not your own. *This is my good news.*

After a last potshot at opponents and grumbling about assorted sorry church members, Paul checks himself, or maybe returns to his main argument, and makes doxology: *To him be the glory forever and always. Amen* (2 Timothy 4:18).

Then he writes,

Say hello to Prisca and Aquila and the household of Onesiphorus. . . . Try hard to come to me before winter. Eubulus, Pudens, Linus, Claudia, and all the brothers and sisters say hello. (2 Timothy 4:19, 21-22)

Little that our people desperately need can be offered by us. We are but heralds, branch managers, the Messiah's emissaries, living reminders. None of us can be their Messiah. So we commend them to the One who gathered us and, love in action, continues to go with us.

At the End, Blessed

You may be a good preacher, an effective, hard-working pastor, but you're not good enough to do something decisive about the specter that most bedevils us—death. All those hortatory, moralistic, sentimental sermons, urging me to be good, to do better, to have a more positive attitude about my contingency, all are quite beside the point, even silly when it comes time for my departing. There's no cure for finitude but God. At the end, if the women running from the tomb on Easter were lying, there's nothing.

So the best you can do for me, at my ending, is to remind me that, in the end, there is the blessing, the benediction of the One who has "pioneered," by going before (Hebrews 12:2). See? His hand is outstretched, inviting himself to go with me, just as he earlier reached toward me in my baptism and vocation. In the end, when all is said and done, which it shall be for me sooner than for you, our sole hope is that the only one who was raised from the dead, who tethered us into ministry, and showed up to help us now and then, shall benevolently take us along with him into his eternity.

Emily Dickinson, characterized her own leaving as reunion:

The Angels bustle in the hall.
Softly my Future climbs the Stair.
I fumble at my Childhood's prayer
So soon to be a Child no more—
Eternity, I'm coming—Sire,
Savior—I've seen the face—before![3]

I guess that's why, in our rituals for death and resurrection, I most love the "committal," the "commendation," at the cemetery. Eulogies extolling the deceased may be of some comfort to a grieving family but mean nothing for the deceased. Exaggerated claims for the pleasing personality or the noble achievements of the person being eulogized are notorious for their prevarication and false presentation of a life. Claim anything you want for the dead; nothing makes them less dead.

Therefore, when we stand beside the open grave and commit the person to God (just like we did at the beginning, in their baptism) we're signaling that the significance of their lives is whatever God says; their future is whatever God makes of it. Just as we have commended them and their future to God at the end of every service on every Sunday. You've seen this face before.

Say hello to Prisca and Aquila and the household of Onesiphorus. Erastus stayed in Corinth, and I left Trophimus in Miletus because of his illness. Try hard to come to me before winter. Eubulus, Pudens, Linus, Claudia, and all the brothers and sisters say hello. The Lord be with your spirit. Grace be with you all (2 Timothy 4:19-22).

Try hard to come to me before winter. Tender, affectionate but perhaps, considering the "winter" that lay ahead for Paul, also poignant. Paul ends his letter with blessing, moving toward winter by reminding Prisca, Aquila, and all the rest that the Lord goes with them into whatever cold dark lies ahead.

May grace be with you all (1 Timothy 6:21).

Blessing upon you for saying yes to Jesus's "Follow me." Though you may have been tempted, you haven't yet abandoned the Stranger on the Shore who came calling to you. Ultimately, it's up to God to bless our ministry, to make something out of our meager efforts to tell the truth and to care for God's people of the truth.

I've been at it for decades, shown up for work, and tried to do my duty. Still, I'm leaving so much good work undone. Vast portions of Scripture remain untouched, passages I've not yet mined and preached, and never will. Wish I could remember the name of the student who, with pathos in her voice, asked such a deep question for which I had no good response. I wonder if she ever got a pastor adept enough to give the answer she deserved. Then there's the young couple's broken marriage I couldn't fix or the guy who showed up at the church door, down on his luck. I shoved him twenty dollars just to keep him from taking my time with his sad story. I could go on.

Oh yes, and the sermons when the congregation generously gave me a hearing only to have me take them down some hermeneutic rabbit hole or lead them haplessly into a blind alley. There was nothing to do with the mess that I dumped on them from the pulpit except to say, "Well, enough for today. Maybe the Lord will figure out how to say what I couldn't. Please rise. I will bless you."

Being forced, by our vocation, to stand before the congregation and bless them, commending them, and all our words and works, to God, is weekly training in the art of dying, in service to the God who slays and makes alive (1 Samuel 2:6-7), gives and takes away (Job 1:21). There's never enough time and breath to complete the work of ministry. Learning, through our ministerial vocation, to live our lives out of our control is dress rehearsal for the ultimate out-of-control experience, *thanatos*. While I still have breath, I'm commissioned by baptism to glorify, enjoy, and to serve God using whatever gifts God has given me in service to God's projects. And when God takes back ░░░░░░░░░ God has loaned to me, I may hope to glorify and enjoy God forever.

Death wisdom makes speculating about your legacy a waste of time. God only knows your work's ultimate significance. In even the most well-meaning and earnest ministry, there's still so much unaddressed injustice, unresolved tragedy, and sermons left unsaid. Don't spend much time thinking about it or regret will consume you. Insist that your ministry be validated by its visible results and you'll end up despising alcoholics for their refusal to be helped by you and hating the Smiths for not showing up last Sunday like you asked and they promised.

About the best you can do, at the end of the service or as you draw your last breath, is to hand it all back to the God who handed it to you as you say, *The Lord be with your spirit. Grace be with you all* (2 Timothy 4:22).

I hope that you're not troubled that an old preacher like me has got, for any of my gratitude, also regrets, misgivings, and doubts. In the end, there's nothing to do with the remorse, the questions, and the unknowing but to commit them to God. If even Paul accumulated a list of things he wished he'd said differently, relationships lost, or differences unreconciled, how much more so have I. Nothing to be done but to say, on your way out the door, *The Lord be with your spirit. Grace be with you all* (2 Timothy 4:22).

Christ Pantocrator, Cathedral, Monreale, Sicily

Paul saves to the end talk of his own ending. The first personal pronoun occurs twenty-two times in Second Timothy 4:6-8. Because this most intensely personal paragraph in the whole letter sounds like an addendum, some commentators think it wasn't in Paul's original letter.

I say it sounds like an old guy exiting, talking to a younger colleague still fresh in the fray, trying to be honest about the contingency of ministry.

I'm already being poured out like a sacrifice to God, and the time of my death is near. I have fought the good fight, finished the race, and kept the faith. At last the champion's wreath that is awarded for righteousness is waiting for me. The Lord, who is the righteous judge, is going to give it to me on that day. He's giving it not only to me but also to all those who have set their heart on waiting for his appearance (2 Timothy 4:6-8).

What's left to be said to those we leave but, *The Lord be with your spirit. Grace be with you all.*

By God's grace, we whom death would consign to oblivion, Christ commits to communion. Said Augustine of our ending,

All shall be Amen and Alleluia.
We shall rest and we shall see,
we shall see and we shall know,
we shall know and we shall love,
we shall love and we shall praise,
behold our end which is no end.[4]

The Lord be with your spirit. Grace be with you all.

Eleven on a Saturday night, Sabbath sleep jolted by the phone's ring. A gruff voice, "Preacher, Chief Blue, sorry to bother, but you're needed. Two of your church members, the Browns, are at it again. Tore up the house. Get over to their place soon as you can."

Two of my church members? And what, pray tell, hath Bob and Bonnie's signature domestic strife to do with me? And on a Saturday?

I dressed, sort of, and raced in the dark across town. Two patrol cars, lights flashing, illuminated the lawn. Upturned furniture in the yard. The Browns' Chevrolet parked in the drive, lights on, both doors open, radio blasting.

"Now Bob, Bonnie, you two settle down. And stop firing that gun. You goin' to mess around and hurt somebody," said the chief through his bullhorn.

Two shots rang out from the house, the upstairs bedroom, I guessed.

Two of my church members?

"Preacher, good to see you," the chief greeted me, hunkered down behind his patrol car. "You know Bob and Bonnie. Things build up and then they just kinda' let it all out, sometime in April. Earlier than usual this year. You want to say something to them?" shoving the bullhorn my way. Angry shouts and wails emerged from the house.

"This, this has happened before?" I stuttered, crouching behind the chief, refusing his bullhorn.

"Yep. But only in the spring. As you know. Wish I could get that gun away from 'em."

"Me too," I added.

"Just the way Bob and Bonnie are. I was in high school with both of 'em. They were a mess back then too. Nice enough folks, except when they get wound up on a Saturday night. Right?" The chief was a Baptist. So it was hard to tell if his amiability was sincere.

"Right," I mumble. All I was thinking was, *Two of my church members? Acting like this. In front of God and Baptists.*

Then, for a good ten minutes silence descended. The chief pronounced, "I'd guess they've probably passed out. Let's go in."

I crept behind the police as they approached the house. "Bob? Bonnie?" the chief shouted periodically.

We found the two wearied combatants out for the count on the sofa, amid an apocalyptic scene of broken furniture, dinnerware, and the strong stench of stale cigarettes mixed with beer. They were holding hands.

"Ya'll ought to be ashamed of yourselves," lectured the chief. "City ought not to have to pay for your monkeyshines."

With that, Bob began to stir, turned on his elbows, smiled at us, and said weakly, cheerfully, "Preacher?" and fell back upon the sofa saying, "She coulda' killed me. Had my head caught in the refrigerator . . . her foot on the door. . . . But maybe she didn't mean it."

With that, Bonnie lifted herself up, turned around, stared at the chief, then back at me, confused, and asked, "Preacher, got a cigarette?" before collapsing again on the sofa.

The police helped each to bed, picking their way through the shards of plates and glasses on the floor. I noted an upturned beer can resting on the oversized Bible on the coffee table.

"That ought to hold 'em 'till next April," pronounced the chief as we made our way out. "They're all yours."

I slept not for the rest of the night, tossing and turning, grumbling about the laity in general and determined to remove Bob from the finance committee. I awakened in a foul frame of mind, in no mood to lead the worship of God.

Two of my church members? When Jesus used some preacher before me to fish for people, what was he thinking when he hauled in the likes of Bob and Bonnie? (See Matthew 13:47-50.)

I professionally shoved the previous night from my mind as I led the Eleven O'Clock. In spite of my efforts at amnesia, occasionally, say during the reading of the first lesson, an image of an overturned plate of spaghetti would bring back the whole, horrible embarrassment. "Let us pray" gave me the chance to refocus on something spiritual.

I preached. Maybe from either First or Second Samuel, who knows? I had a headache. We sang the closing hymn and I dutifully stood in the middle of the chancel glumly to give the benediction. As I stretched out my arms to bless, I looked down to my right, second pew from the front. There sat Bonnie and Bob.

The nerve. Usually the two sit tastefully toward the back of the church, as they should. This day, of all mornings, they chose to place themselves at the front, unashamedly before God and everybody. Both smiled, I hope sheepishly. Bob had a large bandage over his left cheek. Bonnie? Wow, makeup does wonders.

There they were, grinning as if nothing were amiss about the evening before, no problem at all with display of themselves before the whole congregation. No apology to me, or to the Lord.

What could I do? No hope of reparation for these two, not a chance of undoing the cataclysm twelve hours ago, certainly no possibility of making either Bob or Bonnie less crazy, even without the booze. What could I do?

I did as I was trained. Out of habit, I stretched out my arms, maybe in imitation of our Lord on his cross, looked the Browns and the congregation in the eye, and said without flinching what the Lord told me to say, "The LORD bless you and protect you. The LORD make his face shine on you and be gracious to you. The LORD lift up his face to you and grant you peace."[5]

Or as Paul put it to Timothy, *The Lord be with your spirit. Grace be with you all.*

NOTES

Introduction

1. While a number of commentaries helped me study First and Second Timothy, most helpful was Thomas G. Long, 1 & 2 Timothy and Titus, *Belief: A Theological Commentary on the Bible* (Louisville: Westminster John Knox Press, 2016).

2. "Dorothy Day: Lecture on Centenary," https://catholicworker.org /ellsberg-centenary-html/.

3. William H. Willimon, *Pastor: The Theology and Practice of Ordained Ministry*, Revised edition (Nashville: Abingdon Press, 2016).

It's a Joy to Be Called

1. Frederick Beuchner, *The Book of Bebb* (San Francisco: Harper & Row, 1972).

2. Barna Group, "A Rapid Decline in Pastoral Security," https://www.barna .com/research/pastoral-security-confidence/.

Changing My Mind

1. W. H. Auden, "The Age of Anxiety," 1947. http://www.abebooks .co.uk/servlet/BookDetailsPL?bi=852635533.

2. Rowan Williams, "Welcome Versus Inclusion: Interview with Rowan Williams," September 6, 2006, https://www.clarion-journal.com/clarion _journal_of_spirit/2006/09/welcome_versus_.html.

3. Willie James Jennings, *After Whiteness: An Education in Belonging* (William B. Eerdmans Publishing Company: Grand Rapids, Michigan, 2020).

Preaching Is the Most Important Thing You Do

1. William Stringfellow, *An Ethic for Christians and Other Aliens in a Strange Land* (Waco, Texas: Word Books, 1973), 142–43.

2. Will Willimon, *Listeners Dare: Hearing God in the Sermon* (Nashville: Abingdon Press, 2022).

3. Alexander Lang, "Departure: Why I Left the Church," https://www.restorativefaith.org/post/departure-why-i-left-the-church.

4. Reinhold Niebuhr, *Leaves from the Notebook of a Tamed Cynic* (Louisville: Westminster John Knox Press, 1990), 27–56.

5. Catherine Mowry LaCugna, *God for Us: The Trinity and the Christian Life* (San Francisco: HarperSanFrancisco, 1973).

6. William H. Willimon, *The Early Sermons of Karl Barth with Commentary by William H. Willimon* (Louisville: Westminster John Knox Press, 2019).

Pastors Are Mission Leaders

1. Will Willimon, *Leading with the Sermon: Preaching as Leadership* (Minneapolis: Fortress Press, 2020), 21–25.

2. Heidi B. Neumark, *Breathing Space: A Spiritual Journey in the South Bronx* (Boston: Beacon Press, 2003).

Evangelists, All

1. Willimon, *Pastor*, 263-64.

2. William H. Willimon, *Acts*, Interpretation: A Bible Commentary for Teaching and Preaching (Louisville: John Knox Press, 1988).

3. Flannery O'Connor, "On Her Own Work," *Mystery and Manners: Occasional Prose*, ed. Sally and Robert Fitzgerald, (New York: Farrar, Straus & Giroux, 1969), 118.

4. Walter Brueggemann, *The Prophetic Imagination* (Minneapolis: The Fortress Press, Second Edition, 1978, 2001), 88–89.

5. St. Basil, in *Wealth and Poverty in Early Church and Society,* ed. Susan R. Holman (Grand Rapids, Michigan: Baker Academic, 2008), 331.

Caring with Jesus

1. Karl A. Menninger, *Whatever Became of Sin?* (Portland, Oregon: Hawthorn Books, 1973). Thomas A. Harris, *I'm OK—You're OK* (New York: Harper & Row, 1967).

2. *The Christian Century*, August 11, 2021, https://www.christiancentury
.org/article/interview/dangers-providing-pastoral-care.

3. Dietrich Bonhoeffer, *Life Together*, trans. John W. Doberstein (London:
SCM Press, 1954), 122.

4. Kate Bowler, *No Cure for Being Human* (New York: Penguin Random
House, 2021), 118. Beverly R. Gaventa, "A Word Out of Season," https://
www.christiancentury.org/article/features/willimon-and-hauerwas-s-out
-scason-words-pastoral-care.

5. Henri J. M. Nouwen, *The Wounded Healer: Ministry in Contemporary
Society* (New York: Image Doubleday, 1972).

Stirring the Pot

1. Karl Barth, *Church Dogmatics*, III, 2, ed. G. W. Bromiley and
T. F. Torrance (Edinburgh: T&T Clark, 1960). Stanley Hauerwas urges all
new pastors to read *Church Dogmatics*, all nine thousand pages of it, in order
to become true pastoral theologians. I agree with that, but don't have the
courage to say it so I relegate it to this endnote.

2. Will Willimon, *Aging: Growing Old in Church* (Grand Rapids: Baker
Academic, 2020), 149.

Hearing and Speaking God's Word

1. Will Willimon, *Preachers Dare: Speaking for God* (Nashville: Abingdon
Press, 2020), 6.

2. Deborah van Deusen Hunsinger, *Theology and Pastoral Counseling:
An Interdisciplinary Approach* (Grand Rapids: Eerdmans, 1995). George
Hunsinger, *How to Read Karl Barth: The Shape of His Theology* (New York:
Oxford University Press, 1991), 234–80.

3. Will Willimon, *Accidental Preacher: A Memoir*, afterword by Kate
Bowler (Grand Rapids: Eerdmans, 2019).

It's About Jesus

1. Robert W. Jenson, *Systematic Theology*, vol. 1: The Triune God (New
York: Oxford University Press, 1997), 63.

2. Flannery O'Connor, *The Habit of Being: Letters of Flannery O'Connor*,
ed. Sally Fitzgerald (New York: Farrar, Straus and Giroux, 1979), 99.

God Be with You

1. O'Connor, *The Habit of Being*, 354.

2. Henri J. M. Nouwen, *The Living Reminder: Service and Prayer in Memory of Jesus Christ* (San Francisco: HarperSanFrancisco, 1977).

3. Emily Dickinson, *The Complete Poems*, ed. Thomas H. Johnson (Boston: Little, Brown, 1960).

4. Saint Augustine, *The City of God against the Pagans*, trans. and ed. R. W. Dyson (New York: Cambridge University Press, 1998), 426.

5. Adapted from "Two People at Prayer," by William H. Willimon, *Stories by Willimon* (Nashville: Abingdon Press, 2020), 112–14.

Will Willimon Books on Ministry
Published by Abingdon Press

A Peculiar Prophet: Will Willimon and the Art of Preaching (eds. Michael A. Turner, William F. Malambri, III)

A Will to Lead and the Grace to Follow: Letters on Leadership from a Peculiar Prophet (Bryan K. Langlands, ed.)

Bishop: The Art of Questioning Authority by an Authority in Question

Calling and Character: Virtues of the Ordained Life

Clergy and Laity Burnout (Lyle E. Schaller, ed.)

Don't Look Back: Methodist Hope for What Comes Next

God Turned Toward Us: The ABCs of Christian Faith

Integrative Preaching: The Pulpit at the Center

Listeners Dare: Hearing God in the Sermon

Pastor: The Theology and Practice of Ordained Ministry

Pastor: A Reader for Ordained Ministry

Preachers Dare: Speaking for God (The Beecher Lectures)

Preaching and Worship in the Small Church (with Robert L. Wilson)

Resident Aliens: Life in the Christian Colony (with Stanley M. Hauerwas)

The Best of Will Willimon: Acting Up in Jesus' Name

The Last Word: Insights about Church and Ministry

The Service of God: Christian Work and Worship

Undone by Easter: Keeping Preaching Fresh

Who Lynched Willie Earle? Preaching to Confront Racism

Worship as Pastoral Care

Printed in the USA
CPSIA information can be obtained
at www.ICGtesting.com
LVHW011955181024
793924LV00001B/2

9 781791 033880